CONTEMPORARY WORLD ATLAS

Table of Contents

Published and printed in the United States.
Library of Congress Catalog Number: 95-068745

THE UNIVERSE AND SOLAR SYSTEM

The Milky Way Galaxy

Our star, the Sun, is one of 200 billion stars banded together in the enormous gravitational spiral nebula called the Milky Way Galaxy, which is but one of millions of known galaxies in the universe.

The Milky Way is huge; it would take light — which travels at 186,000 miles per second — 100,000 years to go from one end of the galaxy to the other. In addition to the billions of stars, Earth shares the Milky Way with eight other known planets.

Statistical Data for the Milky Way Galaxy

Diameter: 100,000 light-years

Mass: About 200 billion suns

Distance between spiral arms: 6,500 light years

Thickness of galactic disk: 1,300 light-years

Satellite galaxies: 2 (visible only in the southern sky)

Sun

The Sun's diameter — more than 865,000 miles — is 109 times greater than that of the Earth. Even so, the Sun is actually a fairly small star. Somewhere in the vastness of the universe astronomers have located a star that is 3,500 times larger than the Sun.

Diameter: 865,000 miles (1,392,000 km)
Mass: 333,000 times that of the Earth
Surface temperature: 10,300° F (5,700° C)
Central temperature: 27 million° F (15 million° C)
Composition: 70% hydrogen, 27% helium
Spin (at equator): 26 days, 21 hours

Mercury

Distance from the Sun: 35,985,000 miles (57,909,000 km), or 39% that of the Earth
Diameter: 3,031 miles (4,878 km); or 38% that of the Earth
Average surface temperature: 340° F (171° C)
Atmosphere: Extremely thin, contains helium and hydrogen
Length of day: 58 days, 15 hours, 30 minutes
Length of year: 87.97 days
Satellites: None

Venus

Distance from the Sun: 67,241,000 miles (108,209,000 km), or 72% that of the Earth
Diameter: 7,521 miles (12,104 km), or 95% that of the Earth
Surface temperature: 867° F (464° C)
Surface pressure: 90 times that of the Earth, equivalent to the pressure at a water depth of 3,000 feet (900 meters)
Atmosphere: 96% carbon dioxide
Length of day: 243 days, 14 minutes. The planet spins opposite to the rotation of the Earth.
Length of year: 224.7 days
Satellites: None

Earth

Distance from the Sun: 92,960,000 miles (149,598,000 km)
Diameter: 7,926 miles (12,756 km)
Average surface temperature: 58° F (14° C)
Surface pressure: 1 atmosphere
Atmosphere: 78% nitrogen, 21% oxygen
Length of day: 23 hours, 56 minutes and 4 seconds
Length of year: 365.25 days
Satellites: 1

The Moon

The Moon is the Earth's only natural satellite. About 2,160 miles (3,746 km) across, the Moon is an airless, waterless world just one-fourth the size of the Earth. It circles the planet once every 27 days at an average distance of about 238,000 miles (384,000 km).

Jupiter

By any measure, Jupiter is the solar system's giant. To equal Jupiter's bulk would take 318 Earths. Over 1,300 Earth-sized balls could fit within this enormous planet.

Satellites: 2
Distance from the Sun: 483,631,000 miles (778,292,000 km), or 5.2 times that of the Earth
Diameter: 88,700 miles (142,800 km), or 11.3 times that of the Earth
Temperature at cloud tops: –234° F (–148° C)

Mars

Distance from the Sun: 141,642,000 miles (227,940,000 km), about 1.5 times that of the Earth
Diameter: 4,222 miles (6,794 km), or 53% that of the Earth
Average surface temperature: –13° F (–25° C)
Surface pressure: 0.7% (1/150 th) that of the Earth
Atmosphere: 95% carbon dioxide, 2.7% nitrogen
Length of day: 24 hours, 37 minutes
Length of year: 1 year, 321.73 days

Spatial Relationships of the Sun and the Planets

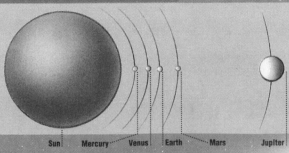

Sun   Mercury   Venus   Earth   Mars   Jupiter   Saturn

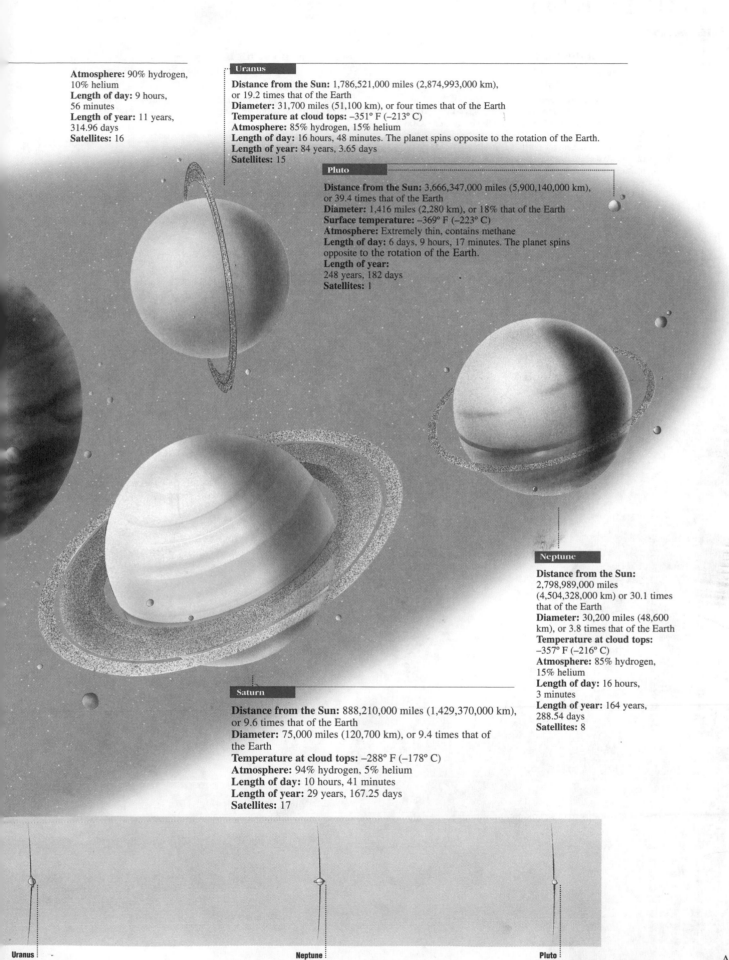

Atmosphere: 90% hydrogen, 10% helium
Length of day: 9 hours, 56 minutes
Length of year: 11 years, 314.96 days
Satellites: 16

Uranus

Distance from the Sun: 1,786,521,000 miles (2,874,993,000 km), or 19.2 times that of the Earth
Diameter: 31,700 miles (51,100 km), or four times that of the Earth
Temperature at cloud tops: −351° F (−213° C)
Atmosphere: 85% hydrogen, 15% helium
Length of day: 16 hours, 48 minutes. The planet spins opposite to the rotation of the Earth.
Length of year: 84 years, 3.65 days
Satellites: 15

Pluto

Distance from the Sun: 3,666,347,000 miles (5,900,140,000 km), or 39.4 times that of the Earth
Diameter: 1,416 miles (2,280 km), or 18% that of the Earth
Surface temperature: −369° F (−223° C)
Atmosphere: Extremely thin, contains methane
Length of day: 6 days, 9 hours, 17 minutes. The planet spins opposite to the rotation of the Earth.
Length of year: 248 years, 182 days
Satellites: 1

Neptune

Distance from the Sun: 2,798,989,000 miles (4,504,328,000 km) or 30.1 times that of the Earth
Diameter: 30,200 miles (48,600 km), or 3.8 times that of the Earth
Temperature at cloud tops: −357° F (−216° C)
Atmosphere: 85% hydrogen, 15% helium
Length of day: 16 hours, 3 minutes
Length of year: 164 years, 288.54 days
Satellites: 8

Saturn

Distance from the Sun: 888,210,000 miles (1,429,370,000 km), or 9.6 times that of the Earth
Diameter: 75,000 miles (120,700 km), or 9.4 times that of the Earth
Temperature at cloud tops: −288° F (−178° C)
Atmosphere: 94% hydrogen, 5% helium
Length of day: 10 hours, 41 minutes
Length of year: 29 years, 167.25 days
Satellites: 17

Uranus   Neptune   Pluto

THE EARTH

History of the Earth

Estimated age of the Earth:
At least 4.6 billion (4,600,000,000) years.

Formation of the Earth:
It is generally thought that the Earth was formed from a cloud of gas and dust (A) revolving around the early Sun. Gravitational forces pulled the cloud's particles together into an ever denser mass (B), with heavier particles sinking to the center. Heat from radioactive elements caused the materials of the embryonic Earth to melt and gradually settle into core and mantle layers. As the surface cooled, a crust formed. Volcanic activity released vast amounts of steam, carbon dioxide and other gases from the Earth's interior. The steam condensed into water to form the oceans, and the gases, prevented by gravity from escaping, formed the beginnings of the atmosphere (C).

The calm appearance of our planet today (D) belies the intense heat of its interior and the violent tectonic forces which are constantly reshaping its surface.

A

B

C

D

Periods in Earth's history

Earth's history is divided into different **eras**, which are subdivided into **periods**.

The most recent periods are themselves subdivided into **epochs**. The main divisions and subdivisions are shown below.

	Began	Ended	
	(million years ago)		
Precambrian Era			
Archean Period	3,800	2,500	Start of life
Proterozoic Period	2,500	590	Life in the seas
Paleozoic Era			
Cambrian Period	590	500	Sea life
Ordovician Period	505	438	First fishes
Silurian Period	438	408	First land plants
Devonian Period	408	360	Amphibians
Carboniferous Period	360	286	First reptiles
Permian Period	286	248	Spread of reptiles
Mesozoic Era			
Triassic Period	248	213	Reptiles and early mammals
Jurassic Period	213	144	Dinosaurs
Cretaceous Period	144	65	Dinosaurs, dying out at the end
Cenozoic Era			
Tertiary Period			
Paleocene	65	55	Large mammals
Eocene	55	38	Primates begin
Oligocene	38	25	Development of primates
Miocene	25	5	Modern-type animals
Pliocene	5	2	Australopithecus ape, ancestor to the human race
Quaternary Period			
Pleistocene	2	0.01	Ice ages; true humans
Holocene	0.01	Present	Modern humans

Source: *Atlas of the Universe* by Patrick Moore, Reed International Books Limited, 1994.

Internal Structure of the Earth

In its simplest form, the Earth is composed of a crust, a mantle with an upper and lower layer, and a core, which has an inner region.

Temperatures in the Earth increase with depth, as is observed in a deep mine shaft or bore-hole, but the prediction of temperatures within the Earth is made difficult by the fact that different rocks conduct heat at different rates: rock salt, for example, has 10 times the heat conductivity of coal. Also, estimates have to take into account the abundance of heat-generating atoms in a rock. Radioactive atoms are concentrated toward the Earth's surface, so the planet has, in effect, a thermal blanket to keep it warm. The temperature at the center of the Earth is believed to be approximately 5,400° F (3,000° C).

Upper Mantle
415 miles
(667 km) thick

Molten Outer Core
1,405 miles
(2,265 km) thick

Solid Inner Core
1,520 miles
(2,440 km)
in diameter

Atmosphere

Lower Mantle
1,365 miles
(2,200 km) thick

Solid Crust
0–19 miles
(0–33 km) thick

Chemical composition of the Earth:

The chemical composition of the Earth varies from crust to core. The upper crust of continents, called sial, is mainly granite, rich in aluminum and silicon. Oceanic crust, or sima, is largely basalt, made of magnesium and silicon. The mantle is composed of rocks that are rich in magnesium and iron silicates, whereas the core, it is believed, is made of iron and nickel oxides.

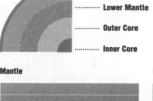

- Sial
- Sima
- Upper Mantle
- Lower Mantle
- Outer Core
- Inner Core

A. Silicon
B. Aluminum
C. Iron
D. Calcium
E. Magnesium
F. Nickel
G. Other

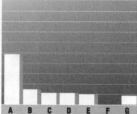

Sial (upper crust of continents)

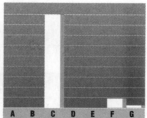

Sima (oceanic crust)

Mantle

Core

(Bar charts with vertical axis labeled % from 0 to 90, horizontal axis labeled A B C D E F G)

Measurements of the Earth

Equatorial circumference of the Earth: 24,901.45 miles (40,066.43 km)

Polar circumference of the Earth: 24,855.33 miles (39,992.22 km)

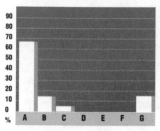

Equatorial diameter of the Earth: 7,926.38 miles (12,753.54 km)

Polar diameter of the Earth: 7,899.80 miles (12,710.77 km)

Equatorial radius of the Earth: 3,963.19 miles (6,376.77 km)

Polar radius of the Earth: 3,949.90 miles (6,355.38 km)

Estimated weight of the Earth:

6,600,000,000,000,000,000,000,000 tons, or 6,600 billion billion tons (5,940 billion billion metric tons)

Total surface area of the Earth: 197,000,000 square miles (510,230,000 sq km)

Total land area of the Earth (including inland water and Antarctica): 57,900,000 square miles (150,100,000 sq km)

Total ocean area of the Earth: 139,200,000 square miles (360,528,000 sq km), or 70% of the Earth's surface area

Total area of the Earth's surface covered with water (oceans and all inland water): 147,750,000 square miles (382,672,500 sq km), or 75% of the Earth's surface area

Types of water: 97% of the Earth's water is salt water; 3% is fresh water

Life on Earth

Number of plant species on Earth: About 350,000

Number of animal species on Earth: More than one million

Estimated total human population of the Earth: 5,628,000,000

Movements of the Earth

Mean distance of the Earth from the Sun: About 93 million miles (149.6 million km)

Period in which the Earth makes one complete orbit around the Sun: 365 days, 5 hours, 48 minutes, and 46 seconds

Speed of the Earth as it orbits the Sun: 66,700 miles (107,320 km) per hour

Period in which the Earth makes one complete rotation on its axis: 23 hours, 56 minutes and 4 seconds

Equatorial speed at which the Earth rotates on its axis: More than 1,000 miles (1,600 km) per hour

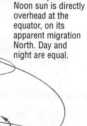

The Shape of the Earth

Comparing the Earth's equatorial and polar dimensions reveals that our planet is actually not a perfect sphere but rather an oblate spheroid, flattened at the poles and bulging at the equator. This is the result of a combination of gravitational and centrifugal forces.

An even more precise term for the Earth's shape is "geoid" — the actual shape of sea level, which is lumpy, with variations away from spheroid of up to 260 feet (80 m). This lumpiness reflects major variations in density in the Earth's outer layers.

The Seasons (Northern Hemisphere)

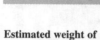

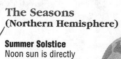

Summer Solstice
Noon sun is directly overhead at 23 1/2° N. Longest day of year.

Vernal Equinox
Noon sun is directly overhead at the equator, on its apparent migration North. Day and night are equal.

Autumnal Equinox
Noon sun is directly overhead at the equator, on its apparent migration South. Day and night are equal.

Winter Solstice
Noon sun is directly overhead at 23 1/2° S. Shortest day of year.

CONTINENTS AND ISLANDS

The word "continents" designates the largest continuous masses of land in the world.

For reasons that are mainly historical, seven continents are generally recognized: Africa, Antarctica, Asia, Australia, Europe, North America, and South America. Since Asia and Europe actually share the same land mass, they are sometimes identified as a single continent, Eurasia.

The lands of the central and south Pacific, including Australia, New Zealand, Micronesia, Melanesia, and Polynesia, are sometimes grouped together as Oceania.

The Continents

Africa

Area in square miles (sq km):
11,700,000 (30,300,000)
Estimated population (Jan. 1, 1995):
697,600,000
Population per square mile (sq km):
60 (23)
Mean elevation in feet (meters):
1,900 (580)
Highest elevation in feet (meters):
Kilimanjaro, Tanzania, 19,340 (5,895)
Lowest elevation in feet (meters):
Lac Assal, Djibouti, 515 (157) below sea level

Antarctica

Area in square miles (sq km):
5,400,000 (14,000,000)
Estimated population (Jan. 1, 1995):
Uninhabited
Population per square mile (sq km):
0 (0)
Mean elevation in feet (meters):
6,000 (1,830)
Highest elevation in feet (meters):
Vinson Massif, 16,066 (4,897)
Lowest elevation in feet (meters):
sea level

Asia

Area in square miles (sq km):
17,300,000 (44,900,000)
Estimated population (Jan. 1, 1995):
3,422,700,000
Population per square mile (sq km):
198 (76)
Mean elevation in feet (meters):
3,000 (910)
Highest elevation in feet (meters):
Mt. Everest, China (Nepal)–Tibet, 29,028 (8,848)
Lowest elevation in feet (meters):
Dead Sea, Israel–Jordan,
1,339 (408) below sea level

Australia

Area in square miles (sq km):
2,966,155 (7,682,300)
Estimated population (Jan. 1, 1995):
18,205,000
Population per square mile (sq km):
6.1 (2.4)
Mean elevation in feet (meters):
1,000 (305)
Highest elevation in feet (meters):
Mt. Kosciusko, New South Wales, 7,310 (2,228)
Lowest elevation in feet (meters):
Lake Eyre, South Australia, 52 (16) below sea level

Europe

Area in square miles (sq km):
3,800,000 (9,900,000)
Estimated population (Jan. 1, 1995):
712,100,000
Population per square mile (sq km):
187 (72)
Mean elevation in feet (meters):
980 (300)
Highest elevation in feet (meters):
Gora El'brus, Russia, 18,510 (5,642)
Lowest elevation in feet (meters):
Caspian Sea, Asia-Europe, 92 (28) below sea level

North America

Area in square miles (sq km):
9,500,000 (24,700,000)
Estimated population (Jan. 1, 1995):
453,300,000
Population per square mile (sq km):
48 (18)
Mean elevation in feet (meters):
2,000 (610)
Highest elevation in feet (meters):
Mt. McKinley, Alaska, U.S., 20,320 (6,194)
Lowest elevation in feet (meters):
Death Valley, California, U.S.,
282 (84) below sea level

Oceania *(incl. Australia)*

Area in square miles (sq km):
3,300,000 (8,500,000)
Estimated population (Jan. 1, 1995):
28,400,000
Population per square mile (sq km):
8.6 (3.3)
Mean elevation in feet (meters):
0 (0)
Highest elevation in feet (meters):
Mt. Wilhelm, Papua New Guinea, 14,793 (4,509)
Lowest elevation in feet (meters):
Lake Eyre, South Australia, 52 (16) below sea level

South America

Area in square miles (sq km):
6,900,000 (17,800,000)
Estimated population (Jan. 1, 1995):
313,900,000
Population per square mile (sq km):
45 (18)
Mean elevation in feet (meters):
1,800 (550)
Highest elevation in feet (meters):
Cerro Aconcagua, Argentina, 22,831 (6,959)
Lowest elevation in feet (meters):
Salinas Chicas, Argentina, 138 (42) below sea level

World

Area in square miles (sq km):
57,900,000 (150,100,000)
Estimated population (Jan. 1, 1995):
5,628,000,000
Population per square mile (sq km):
97 (37)
Mean elevation in feet (meters):
0 (0)
Highest elevation in feet (meters):
Mt. Everest, China–Nepal, 29,028 (8,848)
Lowest elevation in feet (meters):
Dead Sea, Israel–Jordan,
1,339 (408) below sea level

Largest Islands

Rank	Name	Area square miles	Area square km
1	Greenland, North America	840,000	2,175,600
2	New Guinea, Asia-Oceania	309,000	800,000
3	Borneo (Kalimantan), Asia	287,300	744,100
4	Madagascar, Africa	226,500	587,000
5	Baffin Island, Canada	195,928	507,451
6	Sumatra (Sumatera), Indonesia	182,860	473,606
7	Honshū, Japan	89,176	230,966
8	Great Britain, United Kingdom	88,795	229,978
9	Victoria Island, Canada	83,897	217,291
10	Ellesmere Island, Canada	75,767	196,236
11	Celebes (Sulawesi), Indonesia	73,057	189,216
12	South Island, New Zealand	57,708	149,463
13	Java (Jawa), Indonesia	51,038	132,187
14	North Island, New Zealand	44,332	114,821
15	Cuba, North America	42,800	110,800
16	Newfoundland, Canada	42,031	108,860
17	Luzon, Philippines	40,420	104,688
18	Iceland, Europe	39,800	103,000
19	Mindanao, Philippines	36,537	94,630
20	Ireland, Europe	32,600	84,400
21	Hokkaidō, Japan	32,245	83,515
22	Novaya Zemlya, Russia	31,900	82,600
23	Sakhalin, Russia	29,500	76,400
24	Hispaniola, North America	29,400	76,200
25	Banks Island, Canada	27,038	70,028
26	Tasmania, Australia	26,200	67,800
27	Sri Lanka, Asia	24,900	64,600
28	Devon Island, Canada	21,331	55,247
29	Tierra del Fuego, South America	18,600	48,200
30	Kyūshū, Japan	17,129	44,363
31	Melville Island, Canada	16,274	42,149
32	Southampton Island, Canada	15,913	41,214
33	Spitsbergen, Norway	15,260	39,523
34	New Britain, Papua New Guinea	14,093	36,500
35	Taiwan, Asia	13,900	36,000
36	Hainan Dao, China	13,100	34,000
37	Prince of Wales Island, Canada	12,872	33,339
38	Vancouver Island, Canada	12,079	31,285
39	Sicily, Italy	9,926	25,709
40	Somerset Island, Canada	9,570	24,786
41	Sardinia, Italy	9,301	24,090
42	Shikoku, Japan	7,258	18,799
43	Ceram (Seram), Indonesia	7,191	18,625
44	North East Land, Norway	6,350	16,446
45	New Caledonia, Oceania	6,252	16,192
46	Timor, Indonesia	5,743	14,874
47	Flores, Indonesia	5,502	14,250
48	Samar, Philippines	5,100	13,080
49	Negros, Philippines	4,907	12,710
50	Palawan, Philippines	4,550	11,785
51	Panay, Philippines	4,446	11,515
52	Jamaica, North America	4,200	11,000
53	Hawaii, United States	4,034	10,448
54	Cape Breton Island, Canada	3,981	10,311
55	Mindoro, Philippines	3,759	9,735
56	Kodiak Island, United States	3,670	9,505
57	Bougainville, Papua New Guinea	3,600	9,300
58	Cyprus, Asia	3,572	9,251
59	Puerto Rico, North America	3,500	9,100
60	New Ireland, Papua New Guinea	3,500	9,000
61	Corsica (Corse), France	3,367	8,720
62	Crete, Greece	3,189	8,259
63	Vrangelya, Ostrov (Wrangel Island), Russia	2,800	7,300
64	Leyte, Philippines	2,785	7,214
65	Guadalcanal, Solomon Islands	2,060	5,336
66	Long Island, New York, United States	1,377	3,566

Islands, Islands, Everywhere

Four islands — Hokkaidō, Honshū, Kyūshū, and Shikoku —
constitute 98% of Japan's total land area, but the country is actually
comprised of more than 3,000 islands. Similarly, two islands —
Great Britain and Ireland — make up 93% of the total land area of
the British Isles, but the island group also includes more than 5,000
smaller islands.

Greenland

New Guinea

Borneo

Madagascar

Baffin Island

Sumatra

Honshū

Great Britain

Victoria Island

Ellesmere Island

Major World Island Groups

Aleutian Islands (Pacific Ocean)

Alexander Archipelago (Pacific Ocean)

Azores (Atlantic Ocean)

Bahamas (Atlantic Ocean)

Balearic Islands (Mediterranean Sea)

British Isles (Atlantic Ocean)

Bismarck Archipelago (Pacific Ocean)

Canary Islands (Atlantic Ocean)

Cape Verde Islands (Atlantic Ocean)

Dodecanese (Mediterranean Sea)

Faeroe Islands (Atlantic Ocean)

Falkland Islands (Atlantic Ocean)

Fiji Islands (Pacific Ocean)

Galapagos Islands (Pacific Ocean)

Greater Sunda Islands (Indian/Pacific Oceans)

Hawaiian Islands (Pacific Ocean)

Ionian Islands (Mediterranean Sea)

Japan (Pacific Ocean)

Kikládhes (Mediterranean Sea)

Kuril Islands (Pacific Ocean)

Lesser Sunda Islands (Indian Ocean)

Moluccas (Pacific Ocean)

New Hebrides (Atlantic Ocean)

New Siberian Islands (Arctic Ocean)

Novaya Zemlya (Arctic Ocean)

Philippine Islands (Pacific Ocean)

Ryukyu Islands (Pacific Ocean)

Severnaya Zemlya (Arctic Ocean)

Solomon Islands (Pacific Ocean)

Spitsbergen (Arctic Ocean)

Contrasting Population Densities

Some islands are among
the most densely populated
places on Earth, while
others are among the least
densely populated. This
fact is dramatically
illustrated by
the following
comparison of
five islands:

Island	Population per square mile (sq km)
Manhattan, N.Y., U.S., (pop. 1,488,000)	67,636/ sq mile (26,105/ sq km)
Singapore Island, Singapore (pop. 2,921,000)	11,874/ sq mile (4,593/ sq km)
Long Island, N.Y., U.S. (pop. 6,863,000)	4,984/ sq mile (1,925/ sq km)
Baffin Island, Canada (pop. 8,800)	0.04/ sq mile (0.02/ sq km)
Greenland (pop. 57,000)	0.07/ sq mile (0.03/ sq km)

A•7

MOUNTAINS, VOLCANOES, AND EARTHQUAKES

The Tallest Mountain in the World

With its peak reaching 29,028 feet (8,848 m) above sea level, Mt. Everest ranks as the *highest* mountain in the world, but not the *tallest*. That title goes to Mauna Kea, one of the five volcanic mountains that make up the island of Hawaii. From its base on the floor of the Pacific Ocean, Mauna Kea rises 33,476 feet (10,210 m)—more than six miles—although only the top 13,796 feet (4,205 m) are above sea level.

Seafloor Atop Mt. Everest

When Sir Edmund Percival Hillary and Tenzing Norgay reached the summit of Mt. Everest in 1953, they probably did not realize they were standing on the seafloor.

The Himalayan mountain system was formed through the process of plate tectonics. Ocean once separated India and Asia, but 180 million years ago the Indo-Australian crustal plate, on which India sits, began a northward migration and eventually collided with the Eurasian plate. The seafloor between the two landmasses crumpled and was slowly thrust upward. Rock layers that once lay at the bottom of the ocean now crown the peaks of the highest mountains in the world.

Principal Mountains of the World
Δ = *Highest mountain in range, region, country, or state named*

Location	Height Feet	Meters
Africa		
Kilimanjaro, Δ Tanzania (Δ Africa)	19,340	5,895
Kirinyaga (Mount Kenya), Δ Kenya	17,058	5,199
Margherita Peak, Δ Uganda-Δ Zaire	16,763	5,109
Ras Dashen Terara, Δ Ethiopia	15,158	4,620
Meru, Mount, Tanzania	14,978	4,565
Karisimbi, Volcan, Δ Rwanda-Zaire	14,787	4,507
Elgon, Mount, Kenya-Uganda	14,178	4,321
Toubkal, Jebel, Δ Morocco (Δ Atlas Mts.)	13,665	4,165
Cameroon Mountain, Δ Cameroon	13,451	4,100
Antarctica		
Vinson Massif, Δ Antarctica	16,066	4,897
Kirkpatrick, Mount	14,856	4,528
Markham, Mount	14,272	4,350
Jackson, Mount	13,747	4,190
Sidley, Mount	13,717	4,181
Wade, Mount	13,396	4,083
Asia		
Everest, Mount, Δ China-Δ Nepal (Δ Tibet; Δ Himalayas; Δ Asia; Δ World)	29,028	8,848
K2 (Qogir Feng), China-Δ Pakistan (Δ Kashmir; Δ Karakoram Range)	28,250	8,611
Kanchenjunga, Δ India-Nepal	28,208	8,598
Makalu, China-Nepal	27,825	8,481
Dhawlãgiri, Nepal	26,810	8,172
Nanga Parbat, Pakistan	26,660	8,126
Annapurna, Nepal	26,504	8,078
Gasherbrum, China-Pakistan	26,470	8,068
Xixabangma Feng, China	26,286	8,012
Nanda Devi, India	25,645	7,817
Kamet, China-India	25,447	7,756
Namjagbarwa Feng, China	25,446	7,756
Muztag, China (Δ Kunlun Shan)	25,338	7,723
Tirich Mir, Pakistan (Δ Hindu Kush)	25,230	7,690
Gongga Shan, China	24,790	7,556
Kula Kangri, Δ Bhutan	24,784	7,554
Kommunizma, Pik, Δ Tajikistan (Δ Pamir)	24,590	7,495
Nowshak, Δ Afghanistan-Pakistan	24,557	7,485
Pobedy, Pik, China-Russia	24,406	7,439
Chomo Lhari, Bhutan-China	23,997	7,314
Muztag, China	23,891	7,282
Lenina, Pik, Δ Kyrgyzstan-Tajikistan	23,406	7,134
Api, Nepal	23,399	7,132
Kangrinboqê Feng, China	22,028	6,714
Hkakabo Razi, Δ Myanmar	19,296	5,881
Damavend, Qolleh-ye, Δ Iran	18,386	5,604
Agri Dagi (Mount Ararat), Δ Turkey	16,854	5,137
Fuladi, Kuh-e, Afghanistan	16,847	5,135
Jaya, Puncak, Δ Indonesia (Δ New Guinea)	16,503	5,030
Klyuchevskaya Sopka, Vulkan, Russia (Δ Poluostrov Kamchatka)	15,584	4,750
Trikora, Puncak, Indonesia	15,584	4,750
Belucha, Gora, Kazakhstan-Russia	14,783	4,506
Turgen, Mount, Mongolia	14,311	4,362
Kinabalu, Gunong, Δ Malaysia (Δ Borneo)	13,455	4,101
Yü Shan, Δ Taiwan	13,114	3,997
Erciyes Dagi, Turkey	12,851	3,917
Kerinci, Gunung, Indonesia (Δ Sumatra)	12,467	3,800
Fuji, Mt., Δ Japan (Δ Honshu)	12,388	3,776
Rinjani, Gunung, Indonesia (Δ Lombok)	12,224	3,726
Semeru, Gunung, Indonesia (Δ Java)	12,060	3,676
Nabi Shu'ayb, Jabal an-, Δ Yemen (Δ Arabian Peninsula)	12,008	3,660
Australia / Oceania		
Wilhelm, Mt., Δ Papua New Guinea	14,793	4,509
Giluwe, Mt., Papua New Guinea	14,330	4,368
Bangeta, Mt., Papua New Guinea	13,520	4,121
Victoria, Mt., Papua New Guinea (Δ Owen Stanley Range)	13,238	4,035
Cook, Mt., Δ New Zealand (Δ South Island)	12,316	3,754
Europe		
El'brus, Gora, Δ Russia (Δ Caucasus; Δ Europe)	18,510	5,642
Dykhtau, Mt., Russia	17,073	5,204
Blanc, Mont (Monte Bianco) Δ France-Δ Italy (Δ Alps)	15,771	4,807

Location	Height Feet	Meters
Dufourspitze, Italy-Δ Switzerland	15,203	4,634
Weisshorn, Switzerland	14,783	4,506
Matterhorn, Italy-Switzerland	14,692	4,478
Finsteraarhorn, Switzerland	14,022	4,274
Jungfrau, Switzerland	13,642	4,158
Écrins, Barre des, France	13,458	4,102
Viso, Monte, Italy (Δ Cottian Alps)	12,602	3,841
Grossglockner, Δ Austria	12,457	3,797
Teide, Pico de, Δ Spain (Δ Canary Is.)	12,188	3,715
North America		
McKinley, Mt., Δ Alaska (Δ United States; Δ North America)	20,320	6,194
Logan, Mt., Δ Canada (Δ Yukon; Δ St. Elias Mts.)	19,551	5,959
Orizaba, Pico de, Δ Mexico	18,406	5,610
St. Elias, Mt., Alaska-Canada	18,008	5,489
Popocatépetl, Volcán, Mexico	17,930	5,465
Foraker, Mt., Alaska	17,400	5,304
Iztaccíhuatl, Mexico	17,159	5,230
Lucania, Mt., Canada	17,147	5,226
Fairweather, Mt., Alaska-Canada (Δ British Columbia)	15,300	4,663
Whitney, Mt., Δ California	14,494	4,418
Elbert, Mt., Δ Colorado (Δ Rocky Mts.)	14,433	4,399
Massive, Mt., Colorado	14,421	4,396
Harvard, Mt., Colorado	14,420	4,395
Rainier, Mt., Δ Washington (Δ Cascade Range)	14,410	4,392
Williamson, Mt., California	14,370	4,380
La Plata Pk., Colorado	14,361	4,377
Blanca Pk., Colorado (Δ Sangre de Cristo Mts.)	14,345	4,372
Uncompahgre Pk., Colorado (Δ San Juan Mts.)	14,309	4,361
Grays Pk., Colorado (Δ Front Range)	14,270	4,349
Evans, Mt., Colorado	14,264	4,348
Longs Pk., Colorado	14,255	4,345
Wrangell, Mt., Alaska	14,163	4,317
Shasta, Mt., California	14,162	4,317
Pikes Pk., Colorado	14,110	4,301
Colima, Nevado de, Mexico	13,991	4,240
Tajumulco, Volcán, Δ Guatemala (Δ Central America)	13,845	4,220
Gannett Pk., Δ Wyoming	13,804	4,207
Mauna Kea, Δ Hawaii	13,796	4,205
Grand Teton, Wyoming	13,770	4,197
Mauna Loa, Hawaii	13,679	4,169
Kings Pk., Δ Utah	13,528	4,123
Cloud Pk., Wyoming (Δ Bighorn Mts.)	13,167	4,013
Waddington, Mt., Canada (Δ Coast Mts.)	13,163	4,012
Wheeler Pk., Δ New Mexico	13,161	4,011
Boundary Pk., Δ Nevada	13,143	4,006
Robson, Mt., Canada (Δ Canadian Rockies)	12,972	3,954
Granite Pk., Δ Montana	12,799	3,901
Borah Pk., Δ Idaho	12,662	3,859
Humphreys Pk., Δ Arizona	12,633	3,851
Chirripó, Volcán, Δ Costa Rica	12,530	3,819
Columbia, Mt., Canada (Δ Alberta)	12,294	3,747
Adams, Mt., Washington	12,276	3,742
Gunnbjørn Fjeld, Δ Greenland	12,139	3,700
South America		
Aconcagua, Cerro, Δ Argentina (Δ Andes; Δ South America)	22,831	6,959
Ojos del Salado, Nevado, Argentina-Δ Chile	22,615	6,893
Bonete, Cerro, Argentina	22,546	6,872
Huascarán, Nevado, Δ Peru	22,133	6,746
Llullaillaco, Volcán, Argentina-Chile	22,110	6,739
Yerupaja, Nevado, Peru	21,765	6,634
Tupungato, Cerro, Argentina-Chile	21,555	6,570
Sajama, Nevado, Bolivia	21,463	6,542
Illampu, Nevado, Bolivia	21,066	6,421
Illimani, Nevado, Bolivia	20,741	6,322
Chimborazo, Δ Ecuador	20,702	6,310
Antofalla, Volcán, Argentina	20,013	6,100
Cotopaxi, Ecuador	19,347	5,897
Misti, Volcán, Peru	19,101	5,822
Huila, Nevado del, Colombia (Δ Cordillera Central)	18,865	5,750
Bolívar, Pico, Δ Venezuela	16,427	5,007

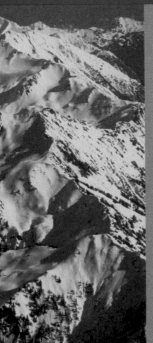

Principal Mountain Systems and Ranges of the World

Alaska Range (North America)
Alps (Europe)
Altai (Asia)
Andes (South America)
Apennines (Europe)
Atlas Mountains (Africa)
Appalachian Mountains (North America)
Brooks Range (North America)
Carpathian Mountains (Europe)
Cascade Range (North America)
Caucasus Mountains (Europe/Asia)
Coast Mountains (North America)
Coast Ranges (North America)
Great Dividing Range (Australia)
Greater Khingan Range (Asia)
Himalayas (Asia)
Hindu Kush (Asia)
Karakoram Range (Asia)
Kunlun Shan (Asia)
Madre Occidental, Sierra (North America)
Madre Oriental, Sierra (North America)
Nevada, Sierra (North America)
Pamir (Asia)
Pyrenees (Europe)
Rocky Mountains (North America)
Sayan Mountains (Asia)
Southern Alps (New Zealand)
Tien Shan (Asia)
Ural Mountains (Europe)
Zagros Mountains (Asia)

Notable Volcanic Eruptions

Year	Volcano Name, Location	Comments
ca. 4895 B.C.	Crater Lake, Oregon, U.S.	Collapse forms caldera that now contains Crater Lake.
ca. 4350 B.C.	Kikai, Ryukyu Islands, Japan	Japan's largest known eruption.
ca. 1628 B.C.	Santorini (Thira), Greece	Eruption devastates late Minoan civilization.
79 A.D.	Vesuvius, Italy	Roman towns of Pompeii and Herculaneum are buried.
ca. 180	Taupo, New Zealand	Area measuring 6,200 square miles (16,000 sq km) is devastated.
ca. 260	Ilopango, El Salvador	Thousands killed, with major impact on Mayan civilization.
915	Towada, Honshu, Japan	Japan's largest historic eruption.
ca. 1000	Baitoushan, China/Korea	Largest known eruption on Asian mainland.
1259	Unknown	Evidence from polar ice cores suggests that a huge eruption, possibly the largest of the millennium, occurred in this year.
1586	Kelut, Java	Explosions in crater lake; mudflows kill 10,000.
1631	Vesuvius, Italy	Eruption kills 4,000.
ca. 1660	Long Island, Papua New Guinea	"The time of darkness" in tribal legends on Papua New Guinea.
1672	Merapi, Java	Pyroclastic flows and mudflows kill 3,000.
1711	Awu, Sangihe Islands, Indonesia	Pyroclastic flows kill 3,000.
1760	Makian, Halmahera, Indonesia	Eruption kills 2,000; island evacuated for seven years.
1772	Papandayan, Java	Debris avalanche causes 2,957 fatalities.
1783	Lakagigar, Iceland	Largest historic lava flows; 9,350 deaths.
1790	Kilauea, Hawaii	Hawaii's last large explosive eruption.
1792	Unzen, Kyushu, Japan	Tsunami and debris avalanche kill 14,500.
1815	Tambora, Indonesia	History's most explosive eruption; 92,000 deaths.
1822	Galunggung, Java	Pyroclastic flows and mudflows kill 4,011.
1856	Awu, Sangihe Islands, Indonesia	Pyroclastic flows kill 2,806.
1883	Krakatau, Indonesia	Caldera collapse; 36,417 people killed, most by tsunami.
1888	Ritter Island, Papua New Guinea	3,000 killed, most by tsunami created by debris avalanche.
1902	Mont Pelee, West Indies	Town of St. Pierre destroyed; 28,000 people killed.
1902	Santa Maria, Guatemala	5,000 killed as 10 villages are buried by volcanic debris.
1912	Novarupta (Katmai), Alaska	Largest 20th-century eruption.
1914	Lassen, California, U.S.	California's last historic eruption.
1919	Kelut, Java	Mudflows devastate 104 villages and kill 5,110 people.
1930	Merapi, Java	1,369 people are killed as 42 villages are totally or partially destroyed.
1943	Parícutin, Mexico	Fissure in cornfield erupts, building cinder cone 1,500 feet (460 m) high within two years. One of the few volcano births ever witnessed.
1951	Lamington, Papua New Guinea	Pyroclastic flows kill 2,942.
1963	Surtsey, Iceland	Submarine eruption builds new island.
1977	Nyiragongo, Zaire	One of the shortest major eruptions and fastest lava flows ever recorded.
1980	St. Helens, Washington, U.S.	Lateral blast; 230-square-mile (600 sq km) area devastated.
1982	El Chichón, Mexico	Pyroclastic surges kill 1,877.
1985	Ruiz, Colombia	Mudflows kill 23,080.
1991	Pinatubo, Luzon, Philippines	Major eruption in densely populated area prompts evacuation of 250,000 people; fatalities number fewer than 800. Enormous amount of gas released into stratosphere lowers global temperatures for more than a year.
1993	Juan de Fuca Ridge, off the coast of Oregon, U.S.	Deep submarine rift eruptions account for three-fourths of all lava produced; this is one of the very few such eruptions that have been well-documented.

Sources: Smithsonian Institution Global Volcanism Program; Volcanoes of the World, Second Edition, by Tom Simkin and Lee Siebert, Geoscience Press and Smithsonian Institution, 1994.

Eruption of Mt. St. Helens in 1980

Significant Earthquakes through History

Year	Estimated Magnitude	Number of Deaths	Place
365		50,000	Knossos, Crete
844		50,000	Damascus, Syria; Antioch, Turkey
856		150,000	Dāmghān, Kashan, Qumis, Iran
893		150,000	Caucasus region
894		180,000	western India
1042		50,000	Palmyra, Baalbek, Syria
1138		230,000	Aleppo, Gansana, Syria
1139	6.8	300,000	Gandzha, Kiapas, Azerbaijan
1201		50,000	upper Egypt to Syria
1290	6.7	100,000	eastern China
1556		820,000	Shaanxi Province, China
1662		300,000	China
1667	6.9	80,000	Caucasus region, northern Iran
1668		50,000	Shandong Province, China
1693		93,000	Sicily, Italy
1727		77,000	Tabrīz, Iran
1731		100,000	Beijing, China
1739		50,000	China
1755		62,000	Morocco, Portugal, Spain
1780	6.7	100,000	Tabrīz, Iran
1868	7.7	70,000	Ecuador, Colombia
1908	7.5	83,000	Calabria, Messina, Italy
1920	8.5	200,000	Gansu and Shaanxi provinces, China

Year	Estimated Magnitude	Number of Deaths	Place
1923	8.2	142,807	Tokyo, Yokohama, Japan
1927	8.3	200,000	Gansu and Qinghai provinces, China
1932	7.6	70,000	Gansu Province, China
1970	7.8	66,794	northern Peru
1976	7.8	242,000	Tangshan, China
1990	7.7	50,000	northwestern Iran

Some Significant U.S. Earthquakes

Year	Estimated Magnitude	Number of Deaths	Place
1811–12	8.6, 8.4, 8.7	<10	New Madrid, Missouri (series)
1886	7.0	60	Charleston, South Carolina
1906	8.3	3,000	San Francisco, California
1933	6.3	115	Long Beach, California
1946	7.4	5‡	Alaska
1964	8.4	125	Anchorage, Alaska
1971	6.8	65	San Fernando, California
1989	7.1	62	San Francisco Bay Area, California
1994	6.8	58	Northridge, California

‡ A tsunami generated by this earthquake struck Hilo, Hawaii, killing 159 people.
Sources: Lowell S. Whiteside, National Geophysical Data Center; Catalog of Significant Earthquakes 2150 B.C.—1991 A.D. by Paula K. Dunbar, Patricia A. Lockridge, and Lowell S. Whiteside, National Geophysical Data Center, National Oceanic and Atmospheric Administration.

Oceans, Seas, Gulfs, and Bays

	Area		Volume of water		Mean depth		Greatest known depth		
	sq. miles	sq. km.	cubic miles	cubic km.	feet	meters	feet	meters	
Pacific Ocean	63,800,000	165,200,000	169,650,000	707,100,000	12,987	3,957	35,810	10,922	Mariana Trench
Atlantic Ocean	31,800,000	82,400,000	79,199,000	330,100,000	11,821	3,602	28,232	8,610	Puerto Rico Trench
Indian Ocean	28,900,000	74,900,000	68,282,000	284,600,000	12,261	3,736	23,812	7,258	Weber Basin
Arctic Ocean	5,400,000	14,000,000	4,007,000	16,700,000	3,712	1,131	17,897	5,453	Lat. 77° 45'N, long. 175°W
Coral Sea	1,850,000	4,791,000	2,752,000	11,470,000	7,857	2,394	30,079	9,165	
Arabian Sea	1,492,000	3,864,000	2,416,000	10,070,000	8,973	2,734	19,029	5,803	
South China Sea	1,331,000	3,447,000	943,000	3,929,000	3,741	1,140	18,241	5,563	
Caribbean Sea	1,063,000	2,753,000	1,646,000	6,860,000	8,175	2,491	25,197	7,685	Off Cayman Islands
Mediterranean Sea	967,000	2,505,000	901,000	3,754,000	4,916	1,498	16,470	5,023	Off Cape Matapan, Greece
Bering Sea	876,000	2,269,000	911,000	3,796,000	5,382	1,640	25,194	7,684	Off Buldir Island
Bengal, Bay of	839,000	2,173,000	1,357,000	5,616,000	8,484	2,585	17,251	5,261	
Okhotsk, Sea of	619,000	1,603,000	316,000	1,317,000	2,694	821	1,029	3,374	Lat. 146° 10'E, long. 46° 50'N
Norwegian Sea	597,000	1,546,000	578,000	2,408,000	5,717	1,742	13,189	4,022	
Mexico, Gulf of	596,000	1,544,000	560,000	2,332,000	8,205	2,500	14,370	4,382	Sigsbee Deep
Hudson Bay	475,000	1,230,000	22,000	92,000	328	100	850	259	Near entrance
Greenland Sea	465,000	1,204,000	417,000	1,740,000	4,739	1,444	15,899	4,849	
Japan, Sea of	413,000	1,070,000	391,000	1,630,000	5,037	1,535	12,041	3,669	
Arafura Sea	400,000	1,037,000	49,000	204,000	646	197	12,077	3,680	
East Siberian Sea	357,000	926,000	14,000	61,000	216	66	508	155	
Kara Sea	349,000	903,000	24,000	101,000	371	113	2,034	620	
East China Sea	290,000	752,000	63,000	263,000	1,145	349	7,778	2,370	
Banda Sea	268,000	695,000	511,000	2,129,000	10,056	3,064	24,418	7,440	
Baffin Bay	263,000	681,000	142,000	593,000	2,825	861	7,010	2,136	
Laptev Sea	262,000	678,000	87,000	363,000	1,772	540	9,780	2,980	
Timor Sea	237,000	615,000	60,000	250,000	1,332	406	10,863	3,310	
Andaman Sea	232,000	602,000	158,000	660,000	3,597	1,096	13,777	4,198	
Chukchi Sea	228,000	590,000	11,000	45,000	252	77	525	160	
North Sea	214,000	554,000	12,000	52,000	315	96	2,655	809	
Java Sea	185,000	480,000	5,000	22,000	147	45	292	89	
Beaufort Sea	184,000	476,000	115,000	478,000	3,295	1,004	12,245	3,731	
Red Sea	174,000	450,000	60,000	251,000	1,831	558	8,648	2,635	
Baltic Sea	173,000	448,000	5,000	20,000	157	48	1,506	459	
Celebes Sea	168,000	435,000	380,000	1,586,000	11,962	3,645	19,173	5,842	
Black Sea	166,000	431,000	133,000	555,000	3,839	1,170	7,256	2,211	
Yellow Sea	161,000	417,000	4,000	17,000	131	40	344	105	
Sulu Sea	134,000	348,000	133,000	553,000	5,221	1,591	18,300	5,576	
Molucca Sea	112,000	291,000	133,000	554,000	6,242	1,902	16,311	4,970	
Ceram Sea	72,000	187,000	54,000	227,000	3,968	1,209	17,456	5,319	
Flores Sea	47,000	121,000	53,000	222,000	6,003	1,829	16,813	5,123	
Bali Sea	46,000	119,000	12,000	49,000	1,349	411	4,253	1,296	
Savu Sea	41,000	105,000	43,000	178,000	5,582	1,701	11,060	3,370	
White Sea	35,000	91,000	1,000	4,400	161	49	1,083	330	
Azov, Sea of	15,000	40,000	100	400	29	9	46	14	
Marmara, Sea of	4,000	11,000	1,000	4,000	1,171	357	4,138	1,261	

Source: Atlas of World Water Balance, *USSR National Committee for the International Water Decade and UNESCO, 1977.*

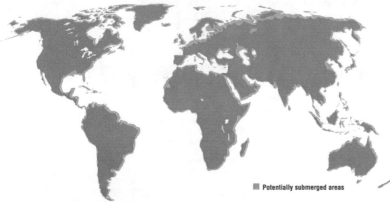

■ Potentially submerged areas

Fluctuating Sea Level

Changes in the Earth's climate have a dramatic effect on the sea level. Only 20,000 years ago, at the height of the most recent ice age, a vast amount of the Earth's water was locked up in ice sheets and glaciers, and the sea level was 330 feet (100 meters) lower than it is today. As the climate warmed slowly, the ice began to melt and the oceans began to rise.

Today there is still a tremendous amount of ice on the Earth. More than nine-tenths of it resides in the enormous ice cap which covers Antarctica. Measuring about 5.4 million square miles (14 million sq km) in surface area, the ice cap is on average one mile (1.6 km) thick but in some places is nearly three miles (4.8 km) thick. If it were to melt, the oceans would rise another 200 feet (60 m), and more than half of the world's population would have to relocate.

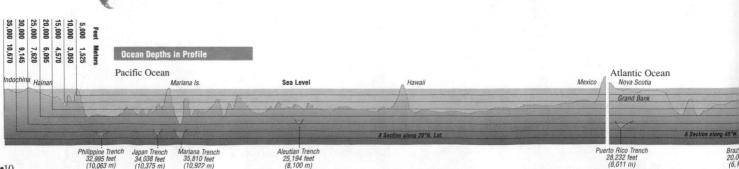

Feet | Meters
35,000 | 10,670
30,000 | 9,145
25,000 | 7,620
20,000 | 6,095
15,000 | 4,570
10,000 | 3,050
5,000 | 1,525

Ocean Depths in Profile

Pacific Ocean

Indochina   Hainan   Mariana Is.   Sea Level   Hawaii   Mexico

Atlantic Ocean
Nova Scotia
Grand Bank

A Section along 20°N. Lat.

A Section along 45°N.

Philippine Trench
32,995 feet
(10,063 m)

Japan Trench
34,038 feet
(10,375 m)

Mariana Trench
35,810 feet
(10,922 m)

Aleutian Trench
25,194 feet
(8,100 m)

Puerto Rico Trench
28,232 feet
(8,611 m)

Braz
20,0
(6,

Deepest Lakes

	Lake	Greatest depth feet	Greatest depth meters
1	Baikal, Lake, Russia	5,315	1,621
2	Tanganyika, Lake, Africa	4,800	1,464
3	Caspian Sea, Asia-Europe	3,363	1,025
4	Nyasa, Lake (Lake Malawi), Malawi-Mozambique-Tanzania	2,317	706
5	Issyk-Kul', Lake, Kyrgyzstan	2,303	702
6	Great Slave Lake, NWT, Canada	2,015	614
7	Matana, Lake, Indonesia	1,936	590
8	Crater Lake, Oregon, U.S.	1,932	589
9	Toba, Lake, Indonesia	1,736	529
10	Sarez, Lake, Tajikistan	1,657	505
11	Tahoe, Lake, California-Nevada, U.S.	1,645	502
12	Kivu, Lake, Rwanda-Zaire	1,628	496
13	Chelan, Lake, Washington, U.S.	1,605	489
14	Quesnel Lake, BC, Canada	1,560	476
15	Adams Lake, BC, Canada	1,500	457

Lakes with the Greatest Volume of Water

	Lake	Volume of water cubic mi	Volume of water cubic km
1	Caspian Sea, Asia-Europe	18,900	78,200
2	Baikal, Lake, Russia	5,500	23,000
3	Tanganyika, Lake, Africa	4,500	18,900
4	Superior, Lake, Canada-U.S.	2,900	12,200
5	Nyasa, Lake (Lake Malawi), Malawi-Mozambique-Tanzania	1,900	7,725
6	Michigan, Lake, U.S.	1,200	4,910
7	Huron, Lake, Canada-U.S.	860	3,580
8	Victoria, Lake, Kenya-Tanzania-Uganda	650	2,700
9	Issyk-Kul', Lake, Kyrgyzstan	415	1,730
10	Ontario, Lake, Canada-U.S.	410	1,710
11	Great Slave Lake, Canada	260	1,070
12	Aral Sea, Kazakhstan-Uzbekistan	250	1,020
13	Great Bear Lake, Canada	240	1,010
14	Ladozhskoye, Ozero, Russia	220	908
15	Titicaca, Lake, Bolivia-Peru	170	710

Sources for volume and depth information: Atlas of World Water Balance, USSR National Committee for the International Water Decade and UNESCO, 1977; Principal Rivers and Lakes of the World, National Oceanic and Atmospheric Administration, 1982.

Principal Lakes

	Lake	Area sq mi	Area sq km
1	Caspian Sea, Asia-Europe	143,240	370,990
2	Superior, Lake, Canada-U.S.	31,700	82,100
3	Victoria, Lake, Kenya-Tanzania-Uganda	26,820	69,463
4	Aral Sea, Kazakhstan-Uzbekistan	24,700	64,100
5	Huron, Lake, Canada-U.S.	23,000	60,000
6	Michigan, Lake, U.S.	22,300	57,800
7	Tanganyika, Lake, Africa	12,350	31,986
8	Baikal, Lake, Russia	12,200	31,500
9	Great Bear Lake, Canada	12,095	31,326
10	Nyasa, Lake (Lake Malawi), Malawi-Mozambique-Tanzania	11,150	28,878
11	Great Slave Lake, Canada	11,030	28,568
12	Erie, Lake, Canada-U.S.	9,910	25,667
13	Winnipeg, Lake, Canada	9,416	24,387
14	Ontario, Lake, Canada-U.S.	7,540	19,529
15	Balkhash, Lake, Kazakhstan	7,100	18,300
16	Ladozhskoye Ozero, Russia	6,833	17,700
17	Chad, Lake (Lac Tchad), Cameroon-Chad-Nigeria	6,300	16,300
18	Onezskoje, Ozero, Russia	3,753	9,720
19	Eyre, Lake, Australia	3,700	9,500
20	Titicaca, Lago, Bolivia-Peru	3,200	8,300
21	Nicaragua, Lago de, Nicaragua	3,150	8,158
22	Mai-Ndombe, Lac, Zaire	3,100	8,000
23	Athabasca, Lake, Canada	3,064	7,935
24	Reindeer Lake, Canada	2,568	6,650
25	Tônlé Sab, Boeng, Cambodia	2,500	6,500
26	Rudolf, Lake, Ethiopia-Kenya	2,473	6,405
27	Issyk-Kul', Ozero, Kyrgyzstan	2,425	6,280
28	Torrens, Lake, Australia	2,300	5,900
29	Albert, Lake, Uganda-Zaire	2,160	5,594
30	Vänern, Sweden	2,156	5,584
31	Nettilling Lake, Canada	2,140	5,542
32	Winnipegosis, Lake, Canada	2,075	5,374
33	Bangweulu, Lake, Zambia	1,930	4,999
34	Nipigon, Lake, Canada	1,872	4,848
35	Urmia, Lake, Iran	1,815	4,701
36	Manitoba, Lake, Canada	1,785	4,624
37	Woods, Lake of the, Canada-U.S.	1,727	4,472
38	Kyoga, Lake, Uganda	1,710	4,429
39	Great Salt Lake, U.S.	1,680	4,351

Lake Baikal

Russia's Great Lake

On a map of the world, Lake Baikal is easy to overlook — a thin blue crescent adrift in the vastness of Siberia. But its inconspicuousness is deceptive, for Baikal is one of the greatest bodies of fresh water on Earth.

Although lakes generally have a life span of less than one million years, Baikal has existed for perhaps as long as 25 million years, which makes it the world's oldest body of fresh water. It formed in a rift that tectonic forces had begun to tear open in the Earth's crust. As the rift grew, so did Baikal. Today the lake is 395 miles (636 km) long and an average of 30 miles (48 km) wide. Only seven lakes in the world have a greater surface area.

Baikal is the world's deepest lake. Its maximum depth is 5,315 feet (1,621 m) — slightly over a mile, and roughly equal to the greatest depth of the Grand Canyon. The lake bottom lies 4,250 feet (1,295 m) below sea level and two-and-a-third miles (3.75 km) below the peaks of the surounding mountains. The crustal rift which Baikal occupies is the planet's deepest land depression, extending to a depth of more than five-and-a-half miles (9 km). The lake sits atop at least four miles (6.4 km) of sediment, the accumulation of 25 million years.

More than 300 rivers empty into Baikal, but only one, the Angara, flows out of it. Despite having only 38% of the surface area of North America's Lake Superior, Baikal contains more water than all five of the Great Lakes combined. Its volume of 5,500 cubic miles (23,000 cubic km) is greater than that of any other freshwater lake in the world and represents approximately one-fifth of all of the Earth's unfrozen fresh water.

Caspian Sea · Lake Superior · Lake Victoria · Aral Sea · Lake Huron · Lake Michigan · Lake Tanganyika · Lake Baikal · Great Bear Lake · Lake Nyasa (Malawi)

France · Mediterranean Sea · Gibraltar · Malta · Israel · Indian Ocean · Sea Level · Sumba · Arctic Ocean · North Pole · 65°N · 65°S · Pacific Ocean · South Pole

A Section along 10°N. Lat.

RIVERS

World's Longest Rivers

Rank	River	Length (Miles)	Length (Kilometers)	Rank	River	Length (Miles)	Length (Kilometers)
1	Nile, Africa	4,145	6,671	36	Amu Darya, Asia	1,578	2,540
2	Amazon-Ucayali, South America	4,000	6,400	37	Murray, Australia	1,566	2,520
3	Yangtze (Chang), Asia	3,900	6,300	38	Ganges, Asia	1,560	2,511
4	Mississippi-Missouri, North America	3,740	6,019	39	Pilcomayo, South America	1,550	2,494
5	Huang (Yellow), Asia	3,395	5,464	40	Euphrates, Asia	1,510	2,430
6	Ob'-Irtysh, Asia	3,362	5,410	41	Ural, Asia	1,509	2,428
7	Río de la Plata-Paraná, South America	3,030	4,876	42	Arkansas, North America	1,459	2,348
8	Congo (Zaïre), Africa	2,900	4,700	43	Colorado, North America (U.S.-Mexico)	1,450	2,334
9	Paraná, South America	2,800	4,500	44	Aldan, Asia	1,412	2,273
10	Amur-Ergun, Asia	2,761	4,444	45	Syr Darya, Asia	1,370	2,205
11	Amur (Heilong), Asia	2,744	4,416	46	Dnieper, Europe	1,350	2,200
12	Lena, Asia	2,700	4,400	47	Araguaia, South America	1,350	2,200
13	Mackenzie, North America	2,635	4,241	48	Cassai (Kasai), Africa	1,338	2,153
14	Mekong, Asia	2,600	4,200	49	Tarim, Asia	1,328	2,137
15	Niger, Africa	2,600	4,200	50	Kolyma, Asia	1,323	2,129
16	Yenisey, Asia	2,543	4,092	51	Orange, Africa	1,300	2,100
17	Missouri-Red Rock, North America	2,533	4,076	52	Negro, South America	1,300	2,100
18	Mississippi, North America	2,348	3,779	53	Ayeyarwady (Irrawaddy), Asia	1,300	2,100
19	Murray-Darling, Australia	2,330	3,750	54	Red, North America	1,270	2,044
20	Missouri, North America	2,315	3,726	55	Juruá, South America	1,250	2,012
21	Volga, Europe	2,194	3,531	56	Columbia, North America	1,240	2,000
22	Madeira, South America	2,013	3,240	57	Xingu, South America	1,230	1,979
23	São Francisco, South America	1,988	3,199	58	Ucayali, South America	1,220	1,963
24	Grande, Rio (Río Bravo), North America	1,885	3,034	59	Saskatchewan-Bow, North America	1,205	1,939
25	Purús, South America	1,860	2,993	60	Peace, North America	1,195	1,923
26	Indus, Asia	1,800	2,900	61	Tigris, Asia	1,180	1,899
27	Danube, Europe	1,776	2,858	62	Don, Europe	1,162	1,870
28	Brahmaputra, Asia	1,770	2,849	63	Songhua, Asia	1,140	1,835
29	Yukon, North America	1,770	2,849	64	Pechora, Europe	1,124	1,809
30	Salween (Nu), Asia	1,750	2,816	65	Kama, Europe	1,122	1,805
31	Zambezi, Africa	1,700	2,700	66	Limpopo, Africa	1,120	1,800
32	Vilyuy, Asia	1,647	2,650	67	Angara, Asia	1,105	1,779
33	Tocantins, South America	1,640	2,639	68	Snake, North America	1,038	1,670
34	Orinoco, South America	1,615	2,600	69	Uruguay, South America	1,025	1,650
35	Paraguay, South America	1,610	2,591	70	Churchill, North America	1,000	1,600

The World's Greatest River

Although the Nile is slightly longer, the Amazon surpasses all other rivers in volume, size of drainage basin, and in nearly every other important category. If any river is to be called the greatest in the world, surely it is the Amazon.

It has been estimated that one-fifth of all of the flowing water on Earth is carried by the Amazon. From its 150-mile (240-km)-wide mouth, the river discharges 6,180,000 cubic feet (174,900 cubic m) of water per second — four-and-a-half times as much as the Congo, ten times as much as the Mississippi, and fifty-six times as much as the Nile. The Amazon's tremendous outflow turns the waters of the Atlantic from salty to brackish for more than 100 miles (160 km) offshore.

Covering more than one-third of the entire continent of South America, the Amazon's vast drainage basin measures 2,669,000 square miles (6,915,000 sq km), nearly twice as large as that of the second-ranked Congo. The Amazon begins its 4,000-mile (6,400-km) journey to the Atlantic from high up in the Andes, only 100 miles (160 km) from the Pacific. Along its course it receives the waters of more than 1,000 tributaries, which rise principally from the Andes, the Guiana Highlands, and the Brazilian Highlands. Seven of the tributaries are more than 1,000 miles (1,600 km) long, and one, the Madeira, is more than 2,000 miles (3,200 km) long.

The depth of the Amazon throughout most of its Brazilian segment exceeds 150 feet (45 m). Depths of more than 300 feet (90 m) have been recorded at points near the mouth. The largest ocean-going vessels can sail as far inland as Manaus, 1,000 miles (1,600 km) from the mouth. Freighters and small passenger vessels can navigate to Iquitos, 2,300 miles (3,700 km) from the mouth, even during times of low water.

Drainage basin of the Amazon River

Rivers with the Greatest Volume of Water

Rank	River Name	Flow of water per second at mouth cubic feet	cubic meters	Rank	River Name	Flow of water per second at mouth cubic feet	cubic meters
1	Amazon, South America	6,180,000	174,900	18	Para-Tocantins, South America (joins Amazon at mouth)	360,000	10,200
2	Congo, Africa	1,377,000	39,000	19	Salween, Asia	353,000	10,000
3	Negro, South America (tributary of Amazon)	1,236,000	35,000	20	Cassai (Kasai), Africa (trib. of Congo)	351,000	9,900
4	Orinoco, South America (trib. of Amazon)	890,000	25,200	21	Mackenzie, North America	343,000	9,700
5	Río de la Plata-Paraná, South America	809,000	22,900	22	Volga, Europe	271,000	7,700
6	Yangtze (Chang), Asia;	770,000	21,800	23	Ohio, North America (trib. of Mississippi)	257,000	7,300
	Madeira, South America (trib. of Amazon)	770,000	21,800	24	Yukon, North America	240,000	6,800
7	Missouri, North America (trib. of Mississippi)	763,000	21,600	25	Indus, Asia	235,000	6,600
8	Mississippi, North America*	640,300	18,100	26	Danube, Europe	227,000	6,400
9	Yenisey, Asia	636,000	18,000	27	Niger, Africa	215,000	6,100
10	Brahmaputra, Asia	575,000	16,300	28	Atchafalaya, North America	181,000	5,100
11	Lena, Asia	569,000	16,100	29	Paraguay, South America	155,000	4,400
12	Zambesi, Africa	565,000	16,000	30	Ob'-Katun, Asia	147,000	4,200
13	Mekong, Asia	500,000	14,100	31	São Francisco, South America	120,000	3,400
14	Saint Lawrence, North America	460,000	13,000	32	Tunguska, Asia	118,000	3,350
15	Ayeyarwady (Irrawaddy), Asia	447,000	12,600	33	Huang (Yellow), Asia	116,000	3,300
16	Ob'-Irtysh, Asia; Ganges, Asia	441,000	12,500	34	Nile, Africa	110,000	3,100
17	Amur, Asia	390,000	11,000				

*Approximately one-third of the Mississippi's water is diverted above Baton Rouge, Louisiana, and reaches the Gulf of Mexico via the Atchafalaya River.

Principal Rivers of the Continents

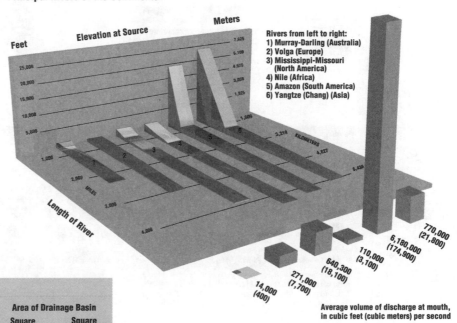

Elevation at Source

Rivers from left to right:
1) Murray-Darling (Australia)
2) Volga (Europe)
3) Mississippi-Missouri (North America)
4) Nile (Africa)
5) Amazon (South America)
6) Yangtze (Chang) (Asia)

Length of River

Average volume of discharge at mouth, in cubic feet (cubic meters) per second

14,000 (400)
271,000 (7,700)
640,300 (18,100)
110,000 (3,100)
6,180,000 (174,900)
770,000 (21,800)

Rivers with the Largest Drainage Basins

Rank	River	Area of Drainage Basin Square Miles	Square Kilometers
1	Amazon, South America	2,669,000	6,915,000
2	Congo (Zaire), Africa	1,474,500	3,820,000
3	Mississippi-Missouri, North America	1,243,000	3,220,000
4	Río de la Plata-Paraná, South America	1,197,000	3,100,000
5	Ob'-Irtysh, Asia	1,154,000	2,990,000
6	Nile, Africa	1,108,000	2,870,000
7	Yenisey-Angara, Asia	1,011,000	2,618,500
8	Lena, Asia	961,000	2,490,000
9	Niger, Africa	807,000	2,090,000
10	Amur-Ergun, Asia	792,000	2,051,300
11	Yangtze (Chang), Asia	705,000	1,826,000
12	Volga, Europe	525,000	1,360,000
13	Zambesi, Africa	513,500	1,330,000
14	St. Lawrence, North America	503,000	1,302,800
15	Huang (Yellow), China	486,000	1,258,700

Sources for volume and drainage basin information: Atlas of World Water Balance, *USSR National Committee for the International Hydrological Decade and UNESCO, 1977;* Principal Rivers and Lakes of the World, *National Oceanic and Atmospheric Administration, 1982.*

CLIMATE AND WEATHER

Temperature Extremes by Continent

Africa
Highest recorded temperature
Al 'Azīzīyah, Libya, September 13, 1922:
136° F (58° C),
Lowest recorded temperature
Ifrane, Morocco, February 11, 1935:
-11° F (-24° C)

Antarctica
Highest recorded temperature
Vanda Station, January 5, 1974:
59° F (15° C)
Lowest recorded temperature
Vostok, July 21, 1983:
-129° F (-89° C)

Asia
Highest recorded temperature
Tirat Zevi, Israel, June 21, 1942:
129° F (54° C)
Lowest recorded temperature
Oymyakon and Verkhoyansk,
Russia, February 5 and 7, 1892,
and February 6, 1933: -90° F (-68° C)

Australia / Oceania
Highest recorded temperature
Cloncurry, Queensland, January 16, 1889:
128° F (53° C)
Lowest recorded temperature
Charlottes Pass, New South Wales,
June 14, 1945, and July 22, 1947: -8° F (-22° C)

Europe
Highest recorded temperature
Sevilla, Spain, August 4, 1881:
122° F (50° C)
Lowest recorded temperature
Ust' Ščugor, Russia, (date not known):
-67° F (-55° C)

North America
Highest recorded temperature
Death Valley, California, United States,
July 10, 1913: 134° F (57° C)
Lowest recorded temperature
Northice, Greenland, January 9, 1954:
-87° F (-66° C)

South America
Highest recorded temperature
Rivadavia, Argentina, December 11, 1905:
120° F (49° C)
Lowest recorded temperature
Sarmiento, Argentina, June 1, 1907:
-27° F (-33° C)

World
Highest recorded temperature
Al 'Azīzīyah, Libya, September 13, 1922:
136° F (58° C)
Lowest recorded temperature
Vostok, Antarctica, July 21, 1983:
-129° F (-89° C)

World Temperature Extremes

Highest mean annual temperature Dalol, Ethiopia, 94° F (34° C)
Lowest mean annual temperature Plateau Station, Antarctica: -70° F (-57° C)

Greatest difference between highest and lowest recorded temperatures
Verkhoyansk, Russia. The highest temperature ever recorded there is 93.5° F (34.2° C); the lowest is -89.7° F (-67.6° C)
— a difference of 183° F (102° C).

Highest temperature ever recorded at the South Pole 7.5° F (-14° C) on December 27, 1978

Most consecutive days with temperatures of 100° F (38° C) or above Marble Bar, Australia, 162 days: October 30, 1923 to April 7, 1924

Greatest rise in temperature within a 12-hour period
Granville, North Dakota, on February 21, 1918. The temperature rose 83° F (46° C), from -33° F (-36° C)
in early morning to +50° F (10° C) in late afternoon

Greatest drop in temperature within a 12-hour period
Fairfield, Montana, on December 24, 1924. The temperature dropped 84° F (46° C), from 63° F (17° C)
at noon to -21° F (-29° C) by midnight

Temperature Ranges for 14 Major Cities around the World

City	Mean Temperature Coldest Winter Month	Mean Temperature Hottest Summer Month	City	Mean Temperature Coldest Winter Month	Mean Temperature Hottest Summer Month
Bombay, India	Jan: 74.3° F (23.5° C)	May: 85.5° F (29.7° C)	Moscow, Russia	Feb: 14.5° F (-9.7° C)	Jul: 65.8° F (18.8° C)
Buenos Aires, Argentina	Aug: 51.3° F (10.7° C)	Jan: 75.0° F (23.9° C)	New York City, U.S.	Jan: 32.9° F (0.5° C)	Jul: 77.0° F (25.0° C)
Calcutta, India	Jan: 67.5° F (19.7° C)	May: 88.5° F (31.4° C)	Osaka, Japan	Jan: 40.6° F (4.8° C)	Aug: 82.2° F (27.9° C)
London, England	Feb: 39.4° F (4.1° C)	Jul: 63.9° F (17.7° C)	Rio de Janeiro, Brazil	Jul: 70.2 ° F (21.2° C)	Jan: 79.9° F (26.6° C)
Los Angeles, U.S.	Jan: 56.3° F (13.5° C)	Jul: 74.1° F (23.4° C)	São Paulo, Brazil	Jul: 58.8° F (14.9° C)	Jan: 71.1° F (21.7° C)
Manila, Philippines	Jan: 77.7° F (25.4° C)	May: 84.9° F (29.4° C)	Seoul, South Korea	Jan: 23.2° F (-4.9° C)	Aug: 77.7° F (25.4° C)
Mexico City, Mexico	Jan: 54.1° F (12.3° C)	May: 64.9° F (18.3° C)	Tokyo, Japan	Jan: 39.6° F (4.2° C)	Aug: 79.3° F (26.3° C)

Precipitation

Greatest local average annual rainfall
Mt. Waialeale, Kauai, Hawaii,
460 inches (1168 cm)

Lowest local average annual rainfall
Arica, Chile, .03 inches (.08 cm)

Greatest rainfall in 12 months
Cherrapunji, India, August 1860 to August 1861:
1,042 inches (2,647 cm)

Greatest rainfall in one month
Cherrapunji, India, July 1861: 366 inches (930 cm)

Greatest rainfall in 24 hours
Cilaos, Reunion, March 15 and 16, 1952:
74 inches (188 cm)

Greatest rainfall in 12 hours
Belouve, Reunion, February 28 and 29, 1964:
53 inches (135 cm)

Most thunderstorms annually
Kampala, Uganda averages 242 days per
year with thunderstorms

Between 1916 and 1920, Bogor, Indonesia
averaged 322 days per year with thunderstorms

Longest dry period
Arica, Chile, October, 1903
to January, 1918 — over 14 years

Largest hailstone ever recorded
Coffeyville, Kansas, U.S., September 3, 1970:
circumference 17.5 inches (44.5 cm)
diameter 5.6 inches (14 cm),
weight 1.67 pounds (758 grams)

Heaviest hailstone ever recorded
Kazakhstan, 1959: 4.18 pounds (1.9 kilograms)

North America's greatest snowfall in one season
Rainier Paradise Ranger Station, Washington,
U.S., 1971–1972: 1,122 inches (2,850 cm)

North America's greatest snowfall in one storm
Mt. Shasta Ski Bowl, California, U.S.,
February 13 to 19, 1959: 189 inches (480 cm)

North America's greatest snowfall in 24 hours
Silver Lake, Colorado, U.S., April 14 and 15, 1921:
76 inches (1 92.5 cm)

N. America's greatest depth of snowfall on the ground
Tamarack, California, U.S., March 11, 1911:
451 inches (1,145.5 cm)

Foggiest place on the U.S. West Coast
Cape Disappointment, Washington,
averages 2,552 hours of fog per year

Foggiest place on the U.S. East Coast
Mistake Island, Maine, averages
1,580 hours of fog per year

Wind

Highest 24-hour mean surface wind speed
Mt. Washington, New Hampshire, U.S.,
April 11 and 12, 1934: 128 mph (206 kph)

Highest 5-minute mean surface wind speed
Mt. Washington, New Hampshire, U.S.,
April 12, 1934: 188 mph (303 kph)

Highest surface wind peak gust:
Mt. Washington, New Hampshire, U.S.,
April 12, 1934: 231 mph (372 kph)

Windiest U.S. Cities

Chicago is sometimes called "The Windy City."
It earned this nickname because of long-winded politicians,
not because it has the strongest gales.

The windiest cities in the U.S. are as follows:

| | Average wind speed | |
Cities	mph	kph
Great Falls, Montana	13.1	21.0
Oklahoma City, Oklahoma	13.0	20.9
Boston, Massachusetts	12.9	20.7
Cheyenne, Wyoming	12.8	20.6
Wichita, Kansas	12.7	20.4

Chicago ranks 16th, with a 10.4 mph (16.7 kph) average.

Deadliest Hurricanes in the U.S. since 1900

Rank	Place	Year	Number of Deaths
1	Texas (Galveston)	1900	>6,000
2	Louisiana	1893	2,000
3	Florida (Lake Okeechobee)	1928	1,836
4	South Carolina, Georgia	1893	>1,000
5	Florida (Keys)	1919	>600
6	New England	1938	600
7	Florida (Keys)	1935	408
8	Southwest Louisiana, north Texas— "Hurricane Audrey"	1957	390
	Northeast U.S.	1944	390
9	Louisiana (Grand Isle)	1909	350
10	Louisana (New Orleans)	1915	275

Tornadoes in the U.S., 1950—1993

Rank	State	Total Number of Tornadoes	Yearly Average	Total Number of Deaths
1	Texas	5,303	120	471
2	Oklahoma	2,259	51	217
3	Kansas	2,068	47	199
4	Florida	1,932	44	81
5	Nebraska	1,618	37	51
	U.S. Total	33,120	753	4,045

Deadliest Floods in the U.S. since 1900

Rank	Place	Year	Number of Deaths
1	Ohio River and tributaries	1913	467
2	Mississippi Valley	1927	313
3	Black Hills, South Dakota	1972	237
4	Texas rivers	1921	215
5	Northeastern U.S., following Hurricane Dianne	1955	187
6	Texas rivers	1913	177
7	James River basin, Virginia	1969	153
8	Big Thompson Canyon, Colorado	1976	139
9	Ohio and Lower Mississippi river basins	1937	137
10	Buffalo Creek, West Virginia	1972	125

POPULATION

During the first two million years of our species' existence, human population grew at a very slow rate, and probably never exceeded 10 million. With the development of agriculture circa 8000 B.C., the growth rate began to rise sharply: by the year A.D. 1, the world population stood at approximately 250 million.

By 1650 the population had doubled to 550 million, and within only 200 years it doubled again, reaching almost 1.2 billion by 1850. Each subsequent doubling has taken only about half as long as the previous one: 100 years to reach 2.5 billion, and 40 years to reach 5.2 billion.

Experts have estimated that today's world population of 5.6 billion represents 5.5% of all of the people who have ever lived on Earth.*

*Population Today, *Population Reference Bureau, February 1995*

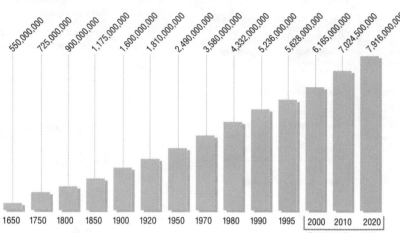

World Population

The World's Estimated Population (as of January 1, 1995): 5,628,000,000
Population Density: 97 people per square mile (37 people per square kilometer)

Historical Populations of the Continents and the World

Year	Africa	Asia	Australia	Europe	North America	Oceania, incl. Australia	South America	World
1650	*100,000,000*	335,000,000	*<1,000,000*	*100,000,000*	*5,000,000*	*2,000,000*	*8,000,000*	*550,000,000*
1750	*95,000,000*	476,000,000	*<1,000,000*	*140,000,000*	*5,000,000*	*2,000,000*	*7,000,000*	*725,000,000*
1800	*90,000,000*	593,000,000	*<1,000,000*	*190,000,000*	*13,000,000*	*2,000,000*	*12,000,000*	*900,000,000*
1850	*95,000,000*	754,000,000	*<1,000,000*	265,000,000	*39,000,000*	*2,000,000*	20,000,000	*1,175,000,000*
1900	*118,000,000*	932,000,000	4,000,000	400,000,000	106,000,000	6,000,000	38,000,000	*1,600,000,000*
1920	*140,000,000*	1,000,000,000	6,000,000	453,000,000	147,000,000	9,000,000	61,000,000	*1,810,000,000*
1950	199,000,000	1,418,000,000	8,000,000	530,000,000	219,000,000	13,000,000	111,000,000	*2,490,000,000*
1970	346,900,000	2,086,200,000	12,460,000	623,700,000	316,600,000	19,200,000	187,400,000	3,580,000,000
1980	463,800,000	2,581,000,000	14,510,000	660,000,000	365,000,000	22,700,000	239,000,000	4,332,000,000
1990	648,300,000	3,156,100,000	16,950,000	688,000,000	423,600,000	26,300,000	293,700,000	5,236,000,000

Figures for years prior to 1970 are rounded to the nearest million. Figures in italics represent rough estimates.

The 50 Most Populous Countries

Rank	Country	Population	Rank	Country	Population	Rank	Country	Population
1	China	1,196,980,000	18	United Kingdom	58,430,000	35	Algeria	27,965,000
2	India	909,150,000	19	Egypt	58,100,000	36	Morocco	26,890,000
3	United States	262,530,000	20	France	58,010,000	37	Sudan	25,840,000
4	Indonesia	193,680,000	21	Italy	57,330,000	38	Korea, North	23,265,000
5	Brazil	159,690,000	22	Ethiopia	55,070,000	39	Peru	23,095,000
6	Russia	150,500,000	23	Ukraine	52,140,000	40	Uzbekistan	22,860,000
7	Pakistan	129,630,000	24	Myanmar	44,675,000	41	Romania	22,745,000
8	Japan	125,360,000	25	Korea, South	44,655,000	42	Venezuela	21,395,000
9	Bangladesh	119,370,000	26	South Africa	44,500,000	43	Nepal	21,295,000
10	Nigeria	97,300,000	27	Zaire	43,365,000	44	Taiwan	21,150,000
11	Mexico	93,860,000	28	Spain	39,260,000	45	Iraq	20,250,000
12	Germany	81,710,000	29	Poland	38,730,000	46	Afghanistan	19,715,000
13	Vietnam	73,760,000	30	Colombia	34,870,000	47	Malaysia	19,505,000
14	Philippines	67,910,000	31	Argentina	34,083,000	48	Uganda	18,270,000
15	Iran	63,810,000	32	Kenya	28,380,000	49	Sri Lanka	18,240,000
16	Turkey	62,030,000	33	Tanzania	28,350,000	50	Australia	18,205,000
17	Thailand	59,870,000	34	Canada	28,285,000			

Most Densely Populated Countries

Rank	Country (Population)	Population per Square Mile	Population per Square Kilometer
1	Monaco (31,000)	44,286	16,316
2	Singapore (2,921,000)	11,874	4,593
3	Vatican City (1,000)	5,000	2,500
4	Malta (368,000)	3,016	1,165
5	Maldives (251,000)	2,183	842
6	Bangladesh (119,370,000)	2,147	829
7	Guernsey (64,000)	2,133	821
8	Bahrain (563,000)	2,109	815
9	Jersey (86,000)	1,911	741
10	Barbados (261,000)	1,572	607
11	Taiwan (21,150,000)	1,522	587
12	Mauritius (1,121,000)	1,423	550
13	Nauru (10,000)	1,235	476
14	Korea, South (44,655,000)	1,168	451
15	Puerto Rico (3,625,000)	1,031	398

Least Densely Populated Countries

Rank	Country (Population)	Population per Square Mile	Population per Square Kilometer
1	Greenland (57,000)	0.07	0.03
2	Mongolia (2,462,000)	4.1	1.6
3	Namibia (1,623,000)	5.1	2.0
4	Mauritania (2,228,000)	5.6	2.2
5	Australia (18,205,000)	6.1	2.4
6	Botswana (1,438,000)	6.4	2.5
7	Iceland (265,000), Suriname (426,000)	6.7	2.6
8	Canada (28,285,000)	7.3	2.8
9	Libya (5,148,000)	7.6	2.9
10	Guyana (726,000)	8.7	3.4
11	Gabon (1,035,000)	10.1	3.9
12	Chad (6,396,000)	12.9	5.0
13	Central African Republic (3,177,000)	13.0	5.1
14	Bolivia (6,790,000)	16.0	6.2
15	Kazakhstan (17,025,000)	16.3	6.3

Most Highly Urbanized Countries

Country	Urban pop. as a % of total pop.
Vatican City	100%
Singapore	100%
Monaco	100%
Belgium	96%
Kuwait	96%
San Marino	92%
Israel (excl. Occupied Areas)	92%
Venezuela	91%
Iceland	91%
Qatar	90%
Uruguay	89%
Netherlands	89%
United Kingdom	89%
Malta	87%
Argentina	86%

Least Urbanized Countries

Country	Urban pop. as a % of total pop.
Bhutan	5%
Burundi	5%
Rwanda	6%
Nepal	11%
Oman	11%
Uganda	11%
Ethiopia	12%
Cambodia (Kampuchea)	12%
Malawi	12%
Burkina Faso	15%
Eritrea	15%
Grenada	15%
Solomon Islands	15%
Bangladesh	16%
Northern Mariana Islands	16%

World's Largest Metropolitan Areas

Rank	Name	Population
1	Tokyo-Yokohama, Japan	30,300,000
2	New York City, U.S.	18,087,000
3	São Paulo, Brazil	16,925,000
4	Osaka-Kobe-Kyoto, Japan	16,900,000
5	Seoul, South Korea	15,850,000
6	Los Angeles, U.S.	14,531,000
7	Mexico City, Mexico	14,100,000
8	Moscow, Russia	13,150,000
9	Bombay, India	12,596,000
10	London, England	11,100,000
11	Rio de Janeiro, Brazil	11,050,000
12	Calcutta, India	11,022,000
13	Buenos Aires, Argentina	11,000,000
14	Paris, France	10,275,000
15	Jakarta, Indonesia	10,200,000

Fastest-Growing and Slowest-Growing Countries

A country's rate of natural increase is determined by subtracting the number of deaths from the number of births for a given period. Immigration and emigration are not included in this formulation.

The highest rate of natural increase among major countries today is Syria's 3.74%. At this rate, Syria's 1995 population of 14,100,000 will double in 19 years and triple in 30 years.

In Hungary and Ukraine deaths currently outnumber births, and the two countries share the same negative rate of natural increase, -0.026%, the lowest in the world.

When all of the countries of the world are compared, pronounced regional patterns become apparent. Of the 35 fastest-growing countries, 30 are found in either Africa or the Middle East. Of the 45 slowest-growing countries, 42 are found in Europe.

THE WORLD'S MOST POPULOUS CITIES

The following table lists the most populous cities of the world by continent and in descending order of population. It includes all cities with central city populations of 500,000 or greater. Cities with populations of less than 500,000 but with metropolitan area populations of 1,000,000 or greater have also been included in the table.

The city populations listed are the latest available census figures or official estimates. For a few cities, only unofficial estimates are available. The year in which the census was taken or to which the estimate refers is provided in parentheses preceding the city population. When comparing populations it is important to keep in mind that some figures are more current than others.

Figures in parentheses represent metropolitan area populations — the combined populations of the cities and their suburbs.

The sequence of information in each listing is as follows: city name, country name (metropolitan area population) (date of census or estimate) city population.

The Most Populous City in the World, through History

With more than 30 million people, Japan's Tokyo-Yokohama agglomeration ranks as the most populous metropolitan area in the world today. New York City held this title from the mid-1920's through the mid-1960's. But what city was the most populous in the world five hundred years ago? Five *thousand* years ago?

The following time line represents one expert's attempt to name the cities that have reigned as the most populous in the world since 3200 B.C. The time line begins with Memphis, the capital of ancient Egypt, which was possibly the first city in the world to attain a population of 20,000.

Listed after each city name is the name of the political entity to which the city belonged during the time that it was the most populous city in the world. The name of the modern political entity in which the city, its ruins, or its site is located, where this entity differs from the historic political entity, is listed in parentheses.

For the purpose of this time line, the word "city" is used in the general sense to denote a city, metropolitan area, or urban agglomeration.

It is important to note that reliable census figures are not available for most of the 5,200 years covered by this time line. Therefore the time line is somewhat subjective and conjectural.

Africa

Cairo (Al Qāhirah),
Egypt (9,300,000) ('86) 6,068,695
Kinshasa, Zaire ('86) 3,000,000
Alexandria (Al Iskandarīyah),
Egypt (3,350,000) ('86) 2,926,859
Casablanca (Dar-el-Beida),
Morocco (2,475,000) ('82) 2,139,204
Abidjan, Cote d'Ivoire ('88) 1,929,079
Addis Ababa, Ethiopia (1,990,000) ('90) . . 1,912,500
Giza (Al Jīzah), Egypt ('86) 1,883,189
Algiers (El Djazaïr),
Algeria (2,547,983)('87) 1,507,241
Nairobi, Kenya ('90) 1,505,000
Dakar, Senegal ('88) 1,490,450
Luanda, Angola ('89) 1,459,900
Antananarivo, Madagascar ('88) 1,250,000
Lagos, Nigeria (3,800,000) ('87) 1,213,000
Ibadan, Nigeria ('87) 1,144,000
Dar es Salaam, Tanzania ('85) 1,096,000
Maputo, Mozambique ('89) 1,069,727
Lusaka, Zambia ('90) 982,362
Accra, Ghana (1,390,000) ('87) 949,113
Cape Town,
South Africa (1,900,000) ('91) 854,616
Conakry, Guinea ('86) 800,000
Kampala, Uganda ('91) 773,463
Durban, South Africa (1,740,000) ('91) . . . 715,669
Shubrā al Khaymah, Egypt ('86) 714,594
Johannesburg,
South Africa (4,000,000) ('91) 712,507
Douala, Cameroon ('87) 712,251
Brazzaville, Congo ('89) 693,712
Harare, Zimbabwe (955,000) ('83) 681,000
Bamako, Mali ('87) 658,275
Wahran, Algeria ('87) 628,558
Mogadishu (Muqdisho), Somalia ('84) 600,000
Bangui, Central African Republic ('89) 596,800
Tunis, Tunisia (1,225,000) ('84) 596,654
Soweto, South Africa ('91) 596,632
Tripoli (Tarābulus),
Libya (960,000) ('88) 591,062
Ogbomosho, Nigeria ('87) 582,900
Lubumbashi, Zaire ('84) 564,830
Yaoundé, Cameroon ('87) 560,785
Kano, Nigeria ('87) 538,300
Mombasa, Kenya ('90) 537,000
Cotonou, Benin ('92) 533,212
Omdurman (Umm Durmān),
Sudan ('83) 526,192
Pretoria, South Africa (1,100,000) ('91) . . . 525,583
Rabat, Morocco (980,000) ('82) 518,616
Lomé, Togo ('87) 500,000
N'Djamena, Chad ('88) 500,000
Khartoum (Al Khartūm),
Sudan (1,450,000) ('83) 473,597

Asia

Seoul (Sŏul),
South Korea (15,850,000) ('90) 10,627,790
Bombay, India (12,596,243) ('91) 9,925,891
Jakarta, Indonesia (10,200,000) ('90) . . . 8,227,746
Tōkyō, Japan (30,300,000) ('90) 8,163,573
Shanghai, China (9,300,000) ('88) 7,220,000
Delhi, India (8,419,084) ('91) 7,206,704
Beijing (Peking),
China (7,320,000) ('88) 6,710,000
İstanbul, Turkey (7,550,000) ('90) 6,620,241
Tehrān, Iran (7,550,000) ('86) 6,042,584

Bangkok (Krung Thep),
Thailand (7,060,000) ('91) 5,620,591
Tianjin (Tientsin), China ('88) 4,950,000
Karāchi, Pakistan (5,300,000) ('81) 4,901,627
Calcutta, India (11,021,918) ('91) 4,399,819
Shenyang (Mukden), China ('88) 3,910,000
Madras, India (5,421,985) ('91) 3,841,396
Baghdād, Iraq ('87) 3,841,268
Pusan, South Korea (3,800,000) ('90) . . . 3,797,566
Dhaka (Dacca),
Bangladesh (6,537,308) ('91) 3,637,892
Wuhan, China ('88) 3,570,000
Yokohama, Japan ('90) 3,220,331
Guangzhou (Canton), China ('88) 3,100,000
Hyderābād, India (4,344,437) ('91) 3,043,896
Ahmadābād, India (3,312,216) ('91) 2,876,710
Thanh Pho Ho Chi Minh (Saigon),
Vietnam (3,300,000) ('89) 2,796,229
Harbin, China ('88) 2,710,000
Lahore, Pakistan (3,025,000) ('81) 2,707,215
T'aipei, Taiwan (6,130,000) ('92) 2,706,453
Singapore, Singapore (3,025,000) ('90) . . 2,690,100
Bangalore, India (4,130,288) ('91) 2,660,088
Ōsaka, Japan (16,900,000) ('90) 2,623,801
Ankara, Turkey (2,650,000) ('90) 2,559,471
Yangon (Rangoon),
Myanmar (2,650,000) ('83) 2,513,023
Chongqing (Chungking), China ('88) 2,502,000
Surabaya, Indonesia ('90) 2,473,272
Nanjing (Nanking), China ('88) 2,390,000
P'yŏngyang, North Korea ('81) 2,355,000
Dalian (Dairen), China ('88) 2,280,000
Taegu, South Korea ('90) 2,228,834
Xi'an (Sian), China ('88) 2,210,000
Nagoya, Japan (4,800,000) ('90) 2,154,793
Tashkent,
Uzbekistan (2,325,000) ('91) 2,113,300
Bandung, Indonesia (2,220,000) ('90) . . . 2,058,122
Chengdu (Chengtu), China ('88) 1,884,000
Kānpur, India (2,029,889) ('91) 1,874,409
Changchun, China ('88) 1,822,000
Inch'ŏn, South Korea ('90) 1,818,293
İzmir, Turkey (1,900,000) ('90) 1,757,414
Medan, Indonesia ('90) 1,730,052
Taiyuan, China ('88) 1,700,000
Sapporo, Japan (1,900,000) ('90) 1,671,742
Quezon City, Philippines ('90) 1,666,766
Nāgpur, India (1,664,006) ('91) 1,624,752
Lucknow, India (1,669,204) ('91) 1,619,115
Manila, Philippines (9,650,000) ('90) 1,598,918
Halab (Aleppo), Syria (1,640,000) ('94) . . 1,591,400
Poona (Pune), India (2,493,987) ('91) . . . 1,566,651
Chittagong, Bangladesh (2,342,662) ('91) 1,566,070
Damascus (Dimashq),
Syria (2,230,000) ('94) 1,549,932
Jinan (Tsinan), China ('88) 1,546,000
New Kowloon (Xinjiulong),
Hong Kong ('86) 1,526,910
Sūrat, India (1,518,950) ('91) 1,498,817
Kōbe, Japan ('90) 1,477,410
Mashhad, Iran ('86) 1,463,508
Kyōto, Japan ('90) 1,461,103
Jaipur, India (1,518,235) ('91) 1,458,483
Novosibirsk, Russia (1,600,000) ('91) . . . 1,446,300
Kābol, Afghanistan ('88) 1,424,400
Kaohsiung, Taiwan (1,845,000) ('92) 1,401,239
Anshan, China ('88) 1,330,000
Kunming, China ('88) 1,310,000
Jiddah, Saudi Arabia ('80) 1,300,000
Qingdao (Tsingtao), China ('88) 1,300,000
Lanzhou (Lanchow), China ('88) 1,297,000
Hangzhou (Hangchow), China ('88) 1,290,000

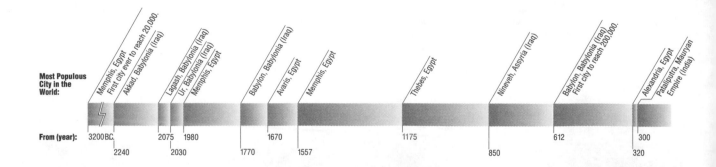

Most Populous City in the World:	Memphis, Egypt First city ever to reach 20,000.	Akkad, Babylonia (Iraq)	Lagash, Babylonia (Iraq)	Ur, Babylonia (Iraq) Memphis, Egypt	Babylon, Babylonia (Iraq)	Avaris, Egypt	Memphis, Egypt	Thebes, Egypt	Nineveh, Assyria (Iraq)	Babylon, Babylonia (Iraq) First city to reach 200,000.	Alexandria, Egypt	Pataliputra, Mauryan Empire (India)
From (year):	3200 B.C.	2240	2075	1980 / 2030	1670 / 1770	1557		1175	850	612	300 / 320	

Fushun (Funan), China ('88) 1,290,000
Tbilisi, Georgia (1,460,000) ('91) 1,279,000
Victoria, Hong Kong (4,770,000) ('91) .. 1,250,993
Riyadh (Ar-Riyād), Saudi Arabia ('80) .. 1,250,000
Semarang, Indonesia ('90) 1,249,230
Fukuoka, Japan (1,750,000) ('90) 1,237,062
Changsha, China ('88) 1,230,000
Shijiazhuang, China ('88) 1,220,000
Jilin (Kirin), China ('88) 1,200,000
Yerevan, Armenia (1,315,000) ('89) ... 1,199,000
Qiqihar (Tsitsihar), China ('88) 1,180,000
Kawasaki, Japan ('90) 1,173,603
Omsk, Russia (1,190,000) ('91) 1,166,800
Alma-Ata (Almaty),
  Kazakhstan (1,190,000) ('91) 1,156,200
Zhengzhou (Chengchow), China ('88) ... 1,150,000
Chelyabinsk, Russia (1,325,000) ('91) .. 1,148,300
Kwangju, South Korea ('90) 1,144,695
Palembang, Indonesia ('90) 1,144,047
Baotou (Paotow), China ('88) 1,130,000
Faisalabad (Lyallpur), Pakistan ('81) .. 1,104,209
Indore, India (1,109,056) ('91) 1,091,674
Nanchang, China ('88) 1,090,000
Hiroshima, Japan (1,575,000) ('90) ... 1,085,705
Baku (Bakı),
  Azerbaijan (2,020,000) ('91) 1,080,500
Tangshan, China ('88) 1,080,000
Bhopāl, India ('91) 1,062,771
Taejŏn, South Korea ('90) 1,062,084
Ürümqi, China ('88) 1,060,000
Ludhiāna, India ('91) 1,042,740
Vadodara, India (1,126,824) ('91) 1,031,346
Guiyang (Kweiyang), China ('88) 1,030,000
Kitakyūshū, Japan (1,525,000) ('90) .. 1,026,455
Kalyān, India ('91) 1,014,557
Esfahān, Iran (1,175,000) ('86) 986,753
Tabrīz, Iran ('86) 971,482
Hāora, India ('91) 950,435
Ujungpandang (Makasar), Indonesia ('90) 944,372
Madurai, India (1,085,914) ('91) 940,989

'Ammān, Jordan (1,625,000) ('89) 936,300
Vārānasi (Benares), India (1,030,863) ('91) 929,270
Krasnoyarsk, Russia ('91) 924,400
Kuala Lumpur, Malaysia (1,475,000) ('80) . 919,610
Sendai, Japan (1,175,000) ('90) 918,398
Patna, India (1,099,647) ('91) 917,243
Adana, Turkey ('90) 916,150
Fuzhou, China ('88) 910,000
Ha Noi, Vietnam (1,275,000) ('89) 905,939
Āgra, India (948,063) ('91) 891,790
Wuxi (Wuhsi), China ('88) 880,000
Handan, China ('88) 870,000
Xuzhou (Süchow), China ('88) 860,000
Benxi (Penhsi), China ('88) 860,000
Shīrāz, Iran ('86) 848,289
Zibo (Zhangdian), China ('88) 840,000
Yichun, China ('88) 840,000
Bursa, Turkey ('90) 834,576

Chiba, Japan ('90) 829,455
Coimbatore, India (1,100,746) ('91) 816,321
Datong, China ('88) 810,000
Sakai, Japan ('90) 807,765
Thāna, India ('91) 803,369
Allahābād, India (844,546) ('91) 792,858
T'aichung, Taiwan ('92) 785,182
Kowloon (Jiulong), Hong Kong ('86) ... 774,781
Caloocan, Philippines ('90) 761,011
Luoyang (Loyang), China ('88) 760,000
Meerut, India (849,799) ('91) 753,778
Vishākhapatnam, India (1,057,118) ('91) . 752,037
Jabalpur, India (888,916) ('91) 741,927
Suzhou (Soochow), China ('88) 740,000
Hefei, China ('88) 740,000
Nanning, China ('88) 720,000
Jinzhou (Chinchou), China ('88) 710,000
Amritsar, India ('91) 708,835
Hyderābād, Pakistan (800,000) ('81) ... 702,539
Vijayawāda, India (845,756) ('91) 701,827
Fuxin, China ('88) 700,000
Jixi, China ('88) 700,000
Huainan, China ('88) 700,000
Multān, Pakistan (732,070) ('81) 696,316
Malang, Indonesia ('90) 695,089
T'ainan, Taiwan ('92) 692,116
Gwalior, India (717,780) ('91) 690,765
Ulsan, South Korea ('90) 682,978
Liuzhou, China ('88) 680,000
Hohhot, China ('88) 670,000
Bucheon, South Korea ('90) 667,777
Jodhpur, India ('91) 666,279
Nāshik, India (725,341) ('91) 656,925
Mudanjiang, China ('88) 650,000
Hubli-Dhārwār, India ('91) 648,298
Vladivostok, Russia ('91) 648,000
Suwŏn, South Korea ('90) 644,968
Himş, Syria ('94) 644,204
Irkutsk, Russia ('91) 640,500
Daqing, China ('88) 640,000
Bishkek, Kyrgyzstan ('91) 631,300
Phnum Pénh, Cambodia ('90) 620,000
Xining (Sining), China ('88) 620,000
Farīdābad, India ('91) 617,717
Basra (Al Basrah), Iraq ('85) 616,700
Khabarovsk, Russia ('91) 613,300
Colombo, Sri Lanka (2,050,000) ('89) .. 612,000
Cebu, Philippines (825,000) ('90) 610,417
Karaganda, Kazakhstan ('91) 608,600
Barnaul, Russia (673,000) ('91) 606,800
Solāpur, India (620,846) ('91) 604,215
Gaziantep, Turkey ('90) 603,434
Novokuznetsk, Russia ('91) 601,900
Khulna, Bangladesh (966,096) ('91) ... 601,051
Gujrānwāla, Pakistan (658,753) ('81) .. 600,993
Rānchi, India (614,795) ('91) 599,306
Srīnagar, India (606,002) ('81) 594,775
Okayama, Japan ('90) 593,730
Hegang, China ('86) 588,300
Bareilly, India (617,350) ('91) 587,211
Guwāhāti, India ('91) 584,342
Dushanbe, Tajikistan ('91) 582,400
Ahvāz, Iran ('86) 579,826
Dandong, China ('86) 579,800
Kumamoto, Japan ('90) 579,306
Ulan Bator, Mongolia ('91) 575,000
Aurangābād, India (592,709) ('91) 573,272
Al-Mawşil, Iraq ('85) 570,926
Ningbo, China ('88) 570,000
Cochin, India (1,140,605) ('91) 564,589
Bākhtarān (Kermānshāh), Iran ('86) ... 560,514
Shantou (Swatow), China ('88) 560,000
Rājkot, India (654,490) ('91) 559,407

Mecca (Makkah), Saudi Arabia ('80) 550,000
Qom, Iran ('86) 543,139
Sŏngnam, South Korea ('90) 540,764
T'aipeihsien, Taiwan ('91) 538,954
Kota, India ('91) 537,371
Kagoshima, Japan ('90) 536,752
Hamamatsu, Japan ('90) 534,620
Funabashi, Japan ('90) 533,270
Mandalay, Myanmar ('83) 532,949
Sagamihara, Japan ('90) 531,542
Jerusalem (Yerushalayim) (Al-Quds),
  Israel (560,000) ('91) 524,500
Trivandrum, India (826,225) ('91) 524,006
Changzhou (Changchow), China ('86) ... 522,700
Davao, Philippines ('90) 521,525
Kemerovo, Russia ('91) 520,700
Higashiōsaka, Japan ('90) 518,319

Chŏnju, South Korea ('90) 517,104
Pimpri-Chinchwad, India ('91) 517,083
Tsuen Wan (Quanwan), Hong Kong ('86) .. 514,241
Konya, Turkey ('90) 513,346
Jalandhar, India ('91) 509,510
Beirut (Bayrūt), Lebanon (1,675,000) ('82) 509,000
Peshāwar, Pakistan (566,248) ('81) ... 506,896
Tomsk, Russia ('91) 505,600
Gorakhpur, India ('91) 505,566
Chandīgarh, India (575,829) ('91) 504,094
Surakarta, Indonesia (590,000) ('90) .. 503,827
Zhangjiakou (Kalgan), China ('88) 500,000
Rāwalpindi, Pakistan (1,040,000) ('81) .. 457,091
Tel Aviv-Yafo, Israel (1,735,000) ('91) ... 339,400
Kuwait (Al-Kuwayt),
  Kuwait (1,375,000) ('85) 44,335

Australia and Oceania

Brisbane, Australia (1,334,017) ('91) 751,115
Perth, Australia (1,143,249) ('91) 80,517
Melbourne, Australia (3,022,439) ('91) ... 60,476
Adelaide, Australia (1,023,597) ('91) 14,843
Sydney, Australia (3,538,749) ('91) 13,501

Europe

Moscow (Moskva),
  Russia (13,150,000) ('91) 8,801,500
London, England, U.K. (11,100,000) ('81) 6,574,009
Saint Petersburg (Leningrad),
  Russia (5,525,000) ('91) 4,466,800
Berlin, Germany (4,150,000) ('91) 3,433,695
Madrid, Spain (4,650,000) ('88) 3,102,846
Rome (Roma), Italy (3,175,000) ('91) ... 2,693,383
Kiev (Kyyiv), Ukraine (3,250,000) ('91) .. 2,635,000
Paris, France (10,275,000) ('90) 2,152,423
Bucharest (Bucureşti),
  Romania (2,300,000) ('92) 2,064,474
Budapest, Hungary (2,515,000) ('90) ... 2,016,774
Barcelona, Spain (4,040,000) ('88) 1,714,355
Hamburg, Germany (2,385,000) ('91) ... 1,652,363

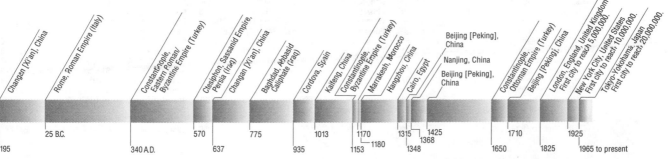

Changan [Xi'an], China — 195
Rome, Roman Empire (Italy) — 25 B.C.
Constantinople, Eastern Roman/Byzantine Empire (Turkey) — 340 A.D.
Ctesiphon, Sassanid Empire, Persia (Iraq) — 570
Changan [Xi'an], China — 637
Baghdad, Abbasid Caliphate (Iraq) — 775
Cordova, Spain — 935
Kaifeng, China — 1013
Constantinople, Byzantine Empire (Turkey) — 1153
Marrakesh, Morocco — 1170 / 1180
Hangzhou, China — 1315
Cairo, Egypt — 1348
Beijing [Peking], China — 1368
Nanjing, China — 1425
Beijing [Peking], China — 1650
Constantinople, Ottoman Empire (Turkey) — 1710
Beijing [Peking], China — 1825
London, England, United Kingdom, First city to reach 5,000,000. — 1925
New York City, United States, First city to reach 10,000,000.
Tokyo-Yokohama, Japan, First city to reach 20,000,000. — 1965 to present

Source: Four Thousand Years of Urban Growth *by Tertius Chandler, Edwin Mellen Press, 1987.*

Warsaw (Warszawa), Poland (2,312,000) ('93) . . . 1,644,500
Minsk, Belarus (1,694,000) ('91) . . . 1,633,600
Kharkiv (Kharkov), Ukraine (2,050,000) ('91) . . . 1,622,800
Vienna (Wien), Austria (1,900,000) ('91) . 1,539,848
Nizhniy Novgorod (Gorky), Russia (2,025,000) ('91) . . . 1,445,000
Yekaterinburg, Russia (1,620,000) ('91) . 1,375,400
Milan (Milano), Italy (3,750,000) ('91) . . 1,371,008
Samara (Kuybyshev), Russia (1,505,000) ('91) . . . 1,257,300
Munich (München), Germany (1,900,000) ('91) . . . 1,229,026
Prague (Praha), Czech Republic (1,328,000) ('91) . . . 1,212,010
Dnipropetrovs'k, Ukraine (1,600,000) ('91) . . . 1,189,300
Sofia (Sofiya), Bulgaria (1,205,000) ('89) 1,136,875
Belgrade (Beograd), Yugoslavia (1,554,826) ('91) . . . 1,136,786
Donets'k, Ukraine (2,125,000) ('91) . . . 1,121,300
Perm', Russia (1,180,000) ('91) . . . 1,110,400
Kazan', Russia (1,165,000) ('91) . . . 1,107,300
Odesa, Ukraine (1,185,000) ('91) . . . 1,100,700
Ufa, Russia (1,118,000) ('91) . . . 1,097,000
Rostov-na-Donu, Russia (1,165,000) ('91) . . . 1,027,600
Naples (Napoli), Italy (2,875,000) ('91) . 1,024,601
Birmingham, England, U.K. (2,675,000) ('81) . . . 1,013,995
Volgograd (Stalingrad), Russia (1,360,000) ('91) . . . 1,007,300
Turin (Torino), Italy (1,550,000) ('91) . . . 961,916
Köln (Cologne), Germany (1,810,000) ('91) 953,551
Łódź, Poland (950,000) ('93) . . . 938,400
Saratov, Russia (1,155,000) ('91) . . . 911,100
Rīga, Latvia (1,005,000) ('91) . . . 910,200
Voronezh, Russia ('91) . . . 900,000
Zaporizhzhya, Ukraine ('91) . . . 896,600
Lisbon (Lisboa), Portugal (2,250,000) ('81) 807,167
L'viv (L'vov), Ukraine ('91) . . . 802,200
Marseille, France (1,225,000) ('90) . . . 800,550
Athens (Athínai), Greece (3,096,775) ('91) . 748,110
Kraków, Poland (823,000) ('93) . . . 744,000
València, Spain (1,270,000) ('88) . . . 743,933
Kryvyy Rih, Ukraine ('91) . . . 724,000
Amsterdam, Netherlands (1,875,000) ('92) . 713,407
Zagreb, Croatia ('87) . . . 697,925
Palermo, Italy ('91) . . . 697,162
Glasgow, Scotland, U.K. (1,800,000) ('90) . 689,210
Chişinău (Kishinev), Moldova ('91) . . . 676,700
Genoa (Genova), Italy (805,000) ('91) . . . 675,639
Stockholm, Sweden (1,491,726) ('91) . . . 674,452
Sevilla, Spain (945,000) ('88) . . . 663,132
Tol'yatti, Russia ('91) . . . 654,700
Ul'yanovsk, Russia ('91) . . . 648,300
Izhevsk, Russia ('91) . . . 646,800
Frankfurt (Frankfurt am Main), Germany (1,935,000) ('91) . . . 644,865
Wrocław (Breslau), Poland ('93) . . . 640,700
Yaroslavl', Russia ('91) . . . 638,100
Krasnodar, Russia ('91) . . . 631,200
Essen, Germany (5,050,000) ('91) . . . 626,973
Dortmund, Germany ('91) . . . 599,055
Vilnius, Lithuania ('92) . . . 596,900
Rotterdam, Netherlands (1,120,000) ('92) . 589,707
Poznań, Poland (666,000) ('93) . . . 582,900
Zaragoza, Spain ('88) . . . 582,239
Stuttgart, Germany (2,005,000) ('91) . . . 579,988
Düsseldorf, Germany (1,225,000) ('91) . . . 575,794
Málaga, Spain ('88) . . . 574,456
Orenburg, Russia ('91) . . . 556,500
Bremen, Germany (790,000) ('91) . . . 551,219
Penza, Russia ('91) . . . 551,100
Tula, Russia (640,000) ('91) . . . 543,600
Liverpool, England, U.K. (1,525,000) ('81) . 538,809
Duisburg, Germany ('91) . . . 535,447
Ryazan', Russia ('91) . . . 527,200
Mariupol' (Zhdanov), Ukraine ('91) . . . 521,800
Hannover, Germany (1,000,000) ('91) . . . 513,010
Astrakhan', Russia ('91) . . . 511,900
Mykolayiv, Ukraine ('91) . . . 511,600
Leipzig, Germany (720,000) ('91) . . . 511,079
Naberezhnyye Chelny, Russia ('91) . . . 510,100
Luhans'k, Ukraine (650,000) ('91) . . . 503,900
Gomel', Belarus ('91) . . . 503,300
Dublin, Ireland (1,140,000) ('86) . . . 502,749

Helsinki (Helsingfors), Finland (1,045,000) ('93) . . . 501,514
Nürnberg, Germany (1,065,000) ('91) . . . 493,692
Antwerpen, Belgium (1,140,000) ('91) . . . 467,518
Copenhagen (København), Denmark (1,670,000) ('92) . . . 464,566
Leeds, England, U.K. (1,540,000) ('81) . . . 445,242
Manchester, England, U.K. (2,775,000) ('81) . . . 437,612
Lyon, France (1,335,000) ('90) . . . 415,487
Katowice, Poland (2,770,000) ('93) . . . 359,900
Porto, Portugal (1,225,000) ('81) . . . 327,368
Mannheim, Germany (1,525,000) ('91) . . . 310,411
Newcastle upon Tyne, England, U.K. (1,300,000) ('81) . . . 199,064
Lille, France (1,050,000) ('90) . . . 172,142
Brussels (Bruxelles), Belgium (2,385,000) ('91) . . . 136,424

North America

Mexico City (Ciudad de México), Mexico (14,100,000) ('90) . . . 8,235,744
New York, N.Y., U.S. (18,087,251) ('90) . 7,322,564
Los Angeles, Ca., U.S. (14,531,529) ('90) 3,485,398
Chicago, Il., U.S. (8,065,633) ('90) . . . 2,783,726
Santo Domingo, Dominican Republic ('90) . . . 2,411,900
Havana (La Habana), Cuba (2,210,000) ('91) . . . 2,119,059
Guadalajara, Mexico (2,325,000) ('90) . . 1,650,042
Houston, Tx., U.S. (3,711,043) ('90) . . . 1,630,553
Philadelphia, Pa., U.S. (5,899,345) ('90) . 1,585,577
Nezahualcóyotl, Mexico ('90) . . . 1,255,456
Ecatepec, Mexico ('90) . . . 1,218,135
San Diego, Ca., U.S. (2,949,000) ('90) . . 1,110,549
Monterrey, Mexico (2,015,000) ('90) . . . 1,068,996
Guatemala, Guatemala (1,400,000) ('89) . 1,057,210
Detroit, Mi., U.S. (4,665,236) ('90) . . . 1,027,974
Montréal, P.Q., Canada (3,127,242) ('91) . 1,017,666
Puebla, Mexico (1,200,000) ('90) . . . 1,007,170
Dallas, Tx., U.S. (3,885,415) ('90) . . . 1,006,877
Phoenix, Az., U.S. (2,122,101) ('90) . . . 983,403
San Antonio, Tx., U.S. (1,302,099) ('90) . . 935,933
Naucalpan de Juárez, Mexico ('90) . . . 845,960
Port-au-Prince, Haiti (880,000) ('87) . . . 797,000
Ciudad Juárez, Mexico ('90) . . . 789,522
San Jose, Ca., U.S. (1,497,577) ('90) . . . 782,248
León, Mexico ('90) . . . 758,279
Baltimore, Md., U.S. (2,382,172) ('90) . . . 736,014
Indianapolis, In., U.S. (1,249,822) ('90) . . 731,327
San Francisco, Ca., U.S. (6,253,311) ('90) . 723,959
Calgary, Ab., Canada (754,033) ('91) . . . 710,677

Tlalnepantla, Mexico ('90) . . . 702,270
Tijuana, Mexico ('90) . . . 698,752
Managua, Nicaragua ('85) . . . 682,000
Zapopan, Mexico ('90) . . . 668,323
Toronto, On., Canada (3,893,046) ('91) . . . 635,395
Jacksonville, Fl., U.S. (906,727) ('90) . . . 635,230
Columbus, Oh., U.S. (1,377,419) ('90) . . . 632,910
Milwaukee, Wi., U.S. (1,607,183) ('90) . . . 628,088
Winnipeg, Mb., Canada (652,354) ('91) . . . 616,790
Edmonton, Ab., Canada (839,924) ('91) . . . 616,741
Memphis, Tn., U.S. (981,747) ('90) . . . 610,337
Washington, D.C., U.S. (3,923,574) ('90) . . 606,900
Kingston, Jamaica (890,000) ('91) . . . 587,798
Tegucigalpa, Honduras ('88) . . . 576,661
Boston, Ma., U.S. (4,171,643) ('90) . . . 574,283
North York, On., Canada ('91) . . . 562,564
Guadalupe, Mexico ('90) . . . 535,332
Scarborough, On., Canada ('91) . . . 524,598
Mérida, Mexico ('90) . . . 523,422
Seattle, Wa., U.S. (2,559,164) ('90) . . . 516,259
Chihuahua, Mexico ('90) . . . 516,153
Acapulco de Juárez, Mexico ('90) . . . 515,374
El Paso, Tx., U.S. (1,211,300) ('90) . . . 515,342
Cleveland, Oh., U.S. (2,759,823) ('90) . . . 505,616
New Orleans, La., U.S. (1,238,816) ('90) . . 496,938
Vancouver, B.C., Canada (1,602,502) ('91) . 471,844
Denver, Co., U.S. (1,848,319) ('90) . . . 467,610
Fort Worth, Tx., U.S. (1,332,053) ('90) . . . 447,619
Portland, Or., U.S. (1,477,895) ('90) . . . 437,319
Kansas City, Mo., U.S. (1,566,280) ('90) . . 435,146
San Juan, Puerto Rico (1,877,000) ('90) . . 426,832
Saint Louis, Mo., U.S. (2,444,099) ('90) . . 396,685
Charlotte, N.C., U.S. (1,162,093) ('90) . . . 395,934
Atlanta, Ga., U.S. (2,833,511) ('90) . . . 394,017
Oakland, Ca., U.S. (2,082,914) ('90) . . . 372,242
Pittsburgh, Pa., U.S. (2,242,798) ('90) . . . 369,879
Sacramento, Ca., U.S. (1,481,102) ('90) . . 369,365
Minneapolis, Mn., U.S. (2,464,124) ('90) . 368,383
Cincinnati, Oh., U.S. (1,744,124) ('90) . . . 364,040
Miami, Fl., U.S. (3,192,582) ('90) . . . 358,548
Buffalo, N.Y., U.S. (1,189,288) ('90) . . . 328,123
Tampa, Fl., U.S. (2,067,959) ('90) . . . 280,015
San José, Costa Rica (1,355,000) ('88) . . . 278,600
Newark, N.J., U.S. (1,824,321) ('90) . . . 275,221
Anaheim, Ca., U.S. (2,410,556) ('90) . . . 266,406
Norfolk, Va., U.S. (1,396,107) ('90) . . . 261,229
Rochester, N.Y., U.S. (1,002,410) ('90) . . . 231,636
Riverside, Ca., U.S. (2,588,793) ('90) . . . 226,505
Orlando, Fl., U.S. (1,072,748) ('90) . . . 164,693
Providence, R.I., U.S. (1,141,510) ('90) . . . 160,728
Salt Lake City, Ut., U.S. (1,072,227) ('90) . 159,936
Fort Lauderdale, Fl., U.S. (1,255,488) ('90) 149,377
Hartford, Ct., U.S. (1,085,837) ('90) . . . 139,739

South America

São Paulo, Brazil (16,925,000) ('91) . . . 9,393,753
Rio de Janeiro, Brazil (11,050,000) ('91) . 5,473,909
Bogotá (Santa Fe de Bogotá), Colombia (4,260,000) ('85) . . . 3,982,941
Buenos Aires, Argentina (11,000,000) ('91) . . . 2,960,976
Salvador, Brazil (2,340,000) ('91) . . . 2,070,296
Caracas, Venezuela (4,000,000) ('90) . . . 1,824,654
Belo Horizonte, Brazil (3,340,000) ('91) . 1,529,566
Brasília, Brazil ('91) . . . 1,513,470
Guayaquil, Ecuador ('90) . . . 1,508,444
Medellín, Colombia (2,095,000) ('85) . . . 1,468,089
Cali, Colombia (1,400,000) ('85) . . . 1,350,565
Recife, Brazil (2,880,000) ('91) . . . 1,296,995
Montevideo, Uruguay (1,550,000) ('85) . 1,251,647
Maracaibo, Venezuela ('90) . . . 1,249,670
Porto Alegre, Brazil (2,850,000) ('91) . . . 1,247,352
Córdoba, Argentina (1,260,000) ('91) . . . 1,148,305
San Justo, Argentina ('91) . . . 1,111,811
Quito, Ecuador (1,300,000) ('90) . . . 1,100,847
Manaus, Brazil ('91) . . . 1,005,634
Goiânia, Brazil (1,130,000) ('91) . . . 912,136
Valencia, Venezuela ('90) . . . 903,621
Barranquilla, Colombia (1,140,000) ('85) . 899,781
Rosario, Argentina (1,190,000) ('91) . . . 894,645
Curitiba, Brazil (1,815,000) ('91) . . . 841,882
Belém, Brazil (1,355,000) ('91) . . . 765,476
Campinas, Brazil (1,290,000) ('91) . . . 759,032
Fortaleza, Brazil (2,040,000) ('91) . . . 743,335
La Paz, Bolivia (1,120,000) ('92) . . . 713,378
Santa Cruz de la Sierra, Bolivia ('92) . . . 697,278
General Sarmiento (San Miguel), Argentina ('91) . . . 646,891
Morón, Argentina ('91) . . . 641,541
Barquisimeto, Venezuela ('90) . . . 625,450
Lomas de Zamora, Argentina ('91) . . . 572,769
Osasco, Brazil ('91) . . . 566,949
Nova Iguaçu, Brazil ('91) . . . 562,062
Teresina, Brazil (665,000) ('91) . . . 556,073
Maceió, Brazil ('91) . . . 554,727
São Bernardo do Campo, Brazil ('91) . . . 550,030
Guarulhos, Brazil ('91) . . . 546,417
Cartagena, Colombia ('85) . . . 531,426
La Plata, Argentina ('91) . . . 520,449
Mar del Plata, Argentina ('91) . . . 519,707
Santo André, Brazil ('91) . . . 518,272
Campo Grande, Brazil ('91) . . . 516,403
Quilmes, Argentina ('91) . . . 509,445
Asunción, Paraguay (700,000) ('92) . . . 502,426
Santos, Brazil (1,165,000) ('91) . . . 415,554
Lima, Perú (4,608,010) ('81) . . . 371,122
Santiago, Chile (4,100,000) ('82) . . . 232,667

COUNTRIES AND FLAGS

This 12-page section presents basic information about each of the world's countries, along with an illustration of each country's flag. A total of 199 countries are listed: the world's 191 fully independent countries, and 8 internally independent countries which are under the protection of other countries in matters of defense and foreign affairs. Colonies and other dependent political entities are not listed.

The categories of information provided for each country are as follows.

Flag: In many countries two or more versions of the national flag exist. For example, there is often a "civil" version which the average person flies, and a "state" version which is flown only at government buildings and government functions. A common difference between the two is the inclusion of a coat of arms on the state version. The flag versions shown here are the ones that each country has chosen to fly at the United Nations.

Country name: The short form of the English translation of the official country name.

Official name: The long form of the English translation of the official country name.

Population: The population figures listed are 1995 estimates based on U.S. census bureau figures and other available information.

Area: Figures provided represent total land area and all inland water. They are based on official data or U.N. data.

Population density: The number of people per square mile and square kilometer, calculated by dividing the country's population figure by its area figure.

Capital: The city that serves as the official seat of government. Population figures follow the capital name. These figures are based upon the latest official data.

AFGHANISTAN
Official Name: Islamic State of
  Afghanistan
Population: 19,715,000
Area: 251,826 sq. mi. (652,225 sq.km.)
Density: 78/sq. mi. (30/sq. km.)
Capital: Kābol (Kabul), 1,424,400

ALGERIA
Official Name: Democratic and
  Popular Republic of Algeria
Population: 27,965,000
Area: 919,595 sq. mi. (2,381,741 sq. km.)
Density: 30/sq. mi. (12/sq. km.)
Capital: Algiers (El Djazaïr),1,507,241

ANGUILLA
Official Name: Anguilla
Population: 7,100
Area: 35 sq. mi. (91 sq. km.)
Density: 203/sq. mi. (78/sq. km.)
Capital: The Valley, 1,042

ALBANIA
Official Name: Republic of Albania
Population: 3,394,000
Area: 11,100 sq. mi. (28,748 sq. km.)
Density: 306/sq. mi. (118/sq. km.)
Capital: Tiranë, 238,100

ANDORRA
Official Name: Principality of Andorra
Population: 59,000
Area: 175 sq. mi. (453 sq. km.)
Density: 337/sq. mi. (130/sq. km.)
Capital: Andorra, 20,437

ANTIGUA AND BARBUDA
Official Name: Antigua and Barbuda
Population: 67,000
Area: 171 sq. mi. (442 sq. km.)
Density: 392/sq. mi. (152/sq. km.)
Capital: St. John's, 24,359

ANGOLA
Official Name: Republic of Angola
Population: 10,690,000
Area: 481,354 sq. mi. (1,246,700 sq.km.)
Density: 22/sq. mi. (8.6/sq. km.)
Capital: Luanda, 1,459,900

Countries
and Flags
continued

BAHAMAS
Official Name: Commonwealth of the
Bahamas
Population: 275,000
Area: 5,382 sq. mi. (13,939 sq. km.)
Pop. Density: 51/sq. mi. (20/sq. km.)
Capital: Nassau, 141,000

BELIZE
Official Name: Belize
Population: 212,000
Area: 8,866 sq. mi. (22,963 sq. km.)
Pop. Density: 24/sq. mi. (9.2/sq. km.)
Capital: Belmopan, 5,256

ARGENTINA
Official Name: Argentine Republic
Population: 34,083,000
Area: 1,073,519 sq. mi. (2,780,400 sq. km.)
Pop. Density: 32/sq. mi. (12/sq. km.)
Capital: Buenos Aires (de facto), 2,960,976,
and Viedma (future), 40,452

BAHRAIN
Official Name: State of Bahrain
Population: 563,000
Area: 267 sq. mi. (691 sq. km.)
Pop. Density: 2,109/sq. mi. (815/sq. km.)
Capital: Al Manāmah, 82,700

BENIN
Official Name: Republic of Benin
Population: 5,433,000
Area: 43,475 sq. mi. (112,600 sq. km.)
Pop. Density: 125/sq. mi. (48/sq. km.)
Capital: Porto-Novo (designated), 164,000,
and Cotonou (de facto), 533,212

ARMENIA
Official Name: Republic of Armenia
Population: 3,794,000
Area: 11,506 sq. mi. (29,800 sq. km.)
Pop. Density: 330/sq. mi. (127/sq. km.)
Capital: Yerevan, 1,199,000

BANGLADESH
Official Name: People's Republic of
Bangladesh
Population: 119,370,000
Area: 55,598 sq. mi. (143,998 sq. km.)
Pop. Density: 2,147/sq. mi. (829/sq. km.)
Capital: Dhaka (Dacca), 3,637,892

BHUTAN
Official Name: Kingdom of Bhutan
Population: 1,758,000
Area: 17,954 sq. mi. (46,500 sq. km.)
Pop. Density: 98/sq. mi. (38/sq. km.)
Capital: Thimphu, 12,000

AUSTRALIA
Official Name: Commonwealth of Australia
Population: 18,205,000
Area: 2,966,155 sq. mi. (7,682,300 sq. km.)
Pop. Density: 6.1/sq. mi. (2.4/sq. km.)
Capital: Canberra, 276,162

BARBADOS
Official Name: Barbados
Population: 261,000
Area: 166 sq. mi. (430 sq. km.)
Pop. Density: 1,572/sq. mi. (607/sq. km.)
Capital: Bridgetown, 5,928

BOLIVIA
Official Name: Republic of Bolivia
Population: 6,790,000
Area: 424,165 sq. mi. (1,098,581 sq. km.)
Pop. Density: 16/sq. mi. (6.2/sq. km.)
Capital: La Paz (seat of government),
713,378, and Sucre (legal capital), 131,769

AUSTRIA
Official Name: Republic of Austria
Population: 7,932,000
Area: 32,377 sq. mi. (83,856 sq. km.)
Pop. Density: 245/sq. mi. (95/sq. km.)
Capital: Vienna (Wien), 1,539,848

BELARUS
Official Name: Republic of Belarus
Population: 10,425,000
Area: 80,155 sq. mi. (207,600 sq. km.)
Pop. Density: 130/sq. mi. (50/sq. km.)
Capital: Minsk, 1,633,600

BOSNIA AND HERZEGOVINA
Official Name: Republic of Bosnia and
Herzegovina
Population: 4,481,000
Area: 19,741 sq. mi. (51,129 sq. km.)
Pop. Density: 227/sq. mi. (88/sq. km.)
Capital: Sarajevo, 341,200

AZERBAIJAN
Official Name: Azerbaijani Republic
Population: 7,491,000
Area: 33,436 sq. mi. (86,600 sq. km.)
Pop. Density: 224/sq. mi. (87/sq. km.)
Capital: Baku (Bakı), 1,080,500

BELGIUM
Official Name: Kingdom of Belgium
Population: 10,075,000
Area: 11,783 sq. mi. (30,518 sq. km.)
Pop. Density: 855/sq. mi. (330/sq. km.)
Capital: Brussels (Bruxelles), 136,424

BOTSWANA
Official Name: Republic of Botswana
Population: 1,438,000
Area: 224,711 sq. mi. (582,000 sq. km.)
Pop. Density: 6.4/sq. mi. (2.5/sq. km.)
Capital: Gaborone, 133,468

BRAZIL
Official Name: Federative Republic of Brazil
Population: 159,690,000
Area: 3,286,500 sq. mi. (8,511,996 sq. km.)
Pop. Density: 49/sq. mi. (19/sq. km.)
Capital: Brasília, 1,513,470

CAMEROON
Official Name: Republic of Cameroon
Population: 13,330,000
Area: 183,568 sq. mi. (475,440 sq. km.)
Pop. Density: 73/sq. mi. (28/sq. km.)
Capital: Yaoundé, 560,785

CHINA
Official Name: People's Republic of China
Population: 1,196,980,000
Area: 3,689,631 sq. mi. (9,556,100 sq. km.)
Pop. Density: 324/sq. mi. (125/sq. km.)
Capital: Beijing (Peking), 6,710,000

BRUNEI
Official Name: Negara Brunei Darussalam
Population: 289,000
Area: 2,226 sq. mi. (5,765 sq. km.)
Pop. Density: 130/sq. mi. (50/sq. km.)
Capital: Bandar Seri Begawan, 22,777

CANADA
Official Name: Canada
Population: 28,285,000
Area: 3,849,674 sq. mi. (9,970,610 sq. km.)
Pop. Density: 7.3/sq. mi. (2.8/sq. km.)
Capital: Ottawa, 313,987

COLOMBIA
Official Name: Republic of Colombia
Population: 34,870,000
Area: 440,831 sq. mi. (1,141,748 sq. km.)
Pop. Density: 79/sq. mi. (31/sq. km.)
Capital: Bogotá, 3,982,941

BULGARIA
Official Name: Republic of Bulgaria
Population: 8,787,000
Area: 42,855 sq. mi. (110,994 sq. km.)
Pop. Density: 205/sq. mi. (79/sq. km.)
Capital: Sofia (Sofiya), 1,136,875

CAPE VERDE
Official Name: Republic of Cape Verde
Population: 429,000
Area: 1,557 sq. mi. (4,033 sq. km.)
Pop. Density: 276/sq. mi. (106/sq. km.)
Capital: Praia, 61,644

COMOROS
Official Name: Federal Islamic Republic of
the Comoros
Population: 540,000
Area: 863 sq. mi. (2,235 sq. km.)
Pop. Density: 626/sq. mi. (242/sq. km.)
Capital: Moroni, 23,432

BURKINA FASO
Official Name: Burkina Faso
Population: 10,275,000
Area: 105,792 sq. mi. (274,000 sq. km.)
Pop. Density: 97/sq. mi. (38/sq. km.)
Capital: Ouagadougou, 441,514

CENTRAL AFRICAN REPUBLIC
Official Name: Central African Republic
Population: 3,177,000
Area: 240,535 sq. mi. (622,984 sq. km.)
Pop. Density: 13/sq. mi. (5.1/sq. km.)
Capital: Bangui, 596,800

CONGO
Official Name: Republic of the Congo
Population: 2,474,000
Area: 132,047 sq. mi. (342,000 sq. km.)
Pop. Density: 19/sq. mi. (7.2/sq. km.)
Capital: Brazzaville, 693,712

BURUNDI
Official Name: Republic of Burundi
Population: 6,192,000
Area: 10,745 sq. mi. (27,830 sq. km.)
Pop. Density: 576/sq. mi. (222/sq. km.)
Capital: Bujumbura, 226,628

CHAD
Official Name: Republic of Chad
Population: 6,396,000
Area: 495,755 sq. mi. (1,284,000 sq. km.)
Pop. Density: 13/sq. mi. (5/sq. km.)
Capital: N'Djamena, 500,000

COOK ISLANDS
Official Name: Cook Islands
Population: 19,000
Area: 91 sq. mi. (236 sq. km.)
Pop. Density: 209/sq. mi. (81/sq. km.)
Capital: Avarua, 10,886

CAMBODIA
Official Name: Kingdom of Cambodia
Population: 9,713,000
Area: 69,898 sq. mi. (181,035 sq. km.)
Pop. Density: 139/sq. mi. (54/sq. km.)
Capital: Phnum Pénh (Phnom Penh), 620,000

CHILE
Official Name: Republic of Chile
Population: 14,050,000
Area: 292,135 sq. mi. (756,626 sq. km.)
Pop. Density: 48/sq. mi. (19/sq. km.)
Capital: Santiago, 232,667

COSTA RICA
Official Name: Republic of Costa Rica
Population: 3,379,000
Area: 19,730 sq. mi. (51,100 sq. km.)
Pop. Density: 171/sq. mi. (66/sq. km.)
Capital: San José, 278,600

Countries
and Flags
continued

CZECH REPUBLIC
Official Name: Czech Republic
Population: 10,430,000
Area: 30,450 sq. mi. (78,864 sq. km.)
Pop. Density: 343/sq. mi. (132/sq. km.)
Capital: Prague (Praha), 1,212,010

EGYPT
Official Name: Arab Republic of Egypt
Population: 58,100,000
Area: 386,662 sq. mi. (1,001,449 sq. km.)
Pop. Density: 150/sq. mi. (58/sq. km.)
Capital: Cairo (Al Qāhirah), 6,068,695

COTE D'IVOIRE
Official Name: Republic of Cote d'Ivoire
Population: 14,540,000
Area: 124,518 sq. mi. (322,500 sq. km.)
Pop. Density: 117/sq. mi. (45/sq. km.)
Capital: Abidjan (de facto), 1,929,079, and
  Yamoussoukro (future), 106,786

DENMARK
Official Name: Kingdom of Denmark
Population: 5,207,000
Area: 16,639 sq. mi. (43,094 sq. km.)
Pop. Density: 313 sq. mi. (121/sq. km.)
Capital: Copenhagen (København), 464,566

EL SALVADOR
Official Name: Republic of El Salvador
Population: 5,280,000
Area: 8,124 sq. mi. (21,041 sq. km.)
Pop. Density: 650/sq. mi. (251/sq. km.)
Capital: San Salvador, 462,652

CROATIA
Official Name: Republic of Croatia
Population: 4,801,000
Area: 21,829 sq. mi. (56,538 sq. km.)
Pop. Density: 220/sq. mi. (85/sq. km.)
Capital: Zagreb, 697,925

DJIBOUTI
Official Name: Republic of Djibouti
Population: 557,000
Area: 8,958 sq. mi. (23,200 sq. km.)
Pop. Density: 62/sq. mi. (24/sq. km.)
Capital: Djibouti, 329,337

EQUATORIAL GUINEA
Official Name: Republic of Equatorial Guinea
Population: 394,000
Area: 10,831 sq. mi. (28,051 sq. km.)
Pop. Density: 36/sq. mi. (14/sq. km.)
Capital: Malabo, 31,630

CUBA
Official Name: Republic of Cuba
Population: 11,560,000
Area: 42,804 sq. mi. (110,861 sq. km.)
Pop. Density: 270/sq. mi. (104/sq. km.)
Capital: Havana (La Habana), 2,119,059

DOMINICA
Official Name: Commonwealth of Dominica
Population: 89,000
Area: 305 sq. mi. (790 sq. km.)
Pop. Density: 292/sq. mi. (113/sq. km.)
Capital: Roseau, 9,348

ERITREA
Official Name: State of Eritrea
Population: 3,458,000
Area: 36,170 sq. mi. (93,679 sq. km.)
Pop. Density: 96/sq. mi. (37/sq. km.)
Capital: Asmera, 358,100

CYPRUS
Official Name: Republic of Cyprus
Population: 551,000
Area: 2,276 sq. mi. (5,896 sq. km.)
Pop. Density: 242/sq. mi. (93/sq. km.)
Capital: Nicosia (Levkosía), 48,221

DOMINICAN REPUBLIC
Official Name: Dominican Republic
Population: 7,896,000
Area: 18,704 sq. mi. (48,442 sq. km.)
Pop. Density: 422/sq. mi. (163/sq. km.)
Capital: Santo Domingo, 2,411,900

ESTONIA
Official Name: Republic of Estonia
Population: 1,515,000
Area: 17,413 sq. mi. (45,100 sq. km.)
Pop. Density: 87/sq. mi. (34/sq. km.)
Capital: Tallinn, 481,500

CYPRUS, NORTH
Official Name: Turkish Republic of
  Northern Cyprus
Population: 182,000
Area: 1,295 sq. mi. (3,355 sq. km.)
Pop. Density: 141/sq. mi. (54/sq. km.)
Capital: Nicosia (Lefkoşa), 37,400

ECUADOR
Official Name: Republic of Ecuador
Population: 11,015,000
Area: 105,037 sq. mi. (272,045 sq. km.)
Pop. Density: 105/sq. mi. (40/sq. km.)
Capital: Quito, 1,100,847

ETHIOPIA
Official Name: Ethiopia
Population: 55,070,000
Area: 446,953 sq. mi. (1,157,603 sq. km.)
Pop. Density: 123/sq. mi. (48/sq. km.)
Capital: Addis Ababa (Adis Abeba), 1,912,500

FIJI
Official Name: Republic of Fiji
Population: 775,000
Area: 7,056 sq. mi. (18,274 sq. km.)
Pop. Density: 110/sq. mi. (42/sq. km.)
Capital: Suva, 69,665

FINLAND
Official Name: Republic of Finland
Population: 5,098,000
Area: 130,559 sq. mi. (338,145 sq. km.)
Pop. Density: 39/sq. mi. (15/sq. km.)
Capital: Helsinki (Helsingfors), 501,514

FRANCE
Official Name: French Republic
Population: 58,010,000
Area: 211,208 sq. mi. (547,026 sq. km.)
Pop. Density: 275/sq. mi. (106/sq. km.)
Capital: Paris, 2,152,423

GABON
Official Name: Gabonese Republic
Population: 1,035,000
Area: 103,347 sq. mi. (267,667 sq. km.)
Pop. Density: 10/sq. mi. (3.9/sq. km.)
Capital: Libreville, 235,700

GAMBIA
Official Name: Republic of the Gambia
Population: 1,082,000
Area: 4,127 sq. mi. (10,689 sq. km.)
Pop. Density: 262/sq. mi. (101/sq. km.)
Capital: Banjul, 44,188

GEORGIA
Official Name: Republic of Georgia
Population: 5,704,000
Area: 26,911 sq. mi. (69,700 sq. km.)
Pop. Density: 212/sq. mi. (82/sq. km.)
Capital: Tbilisi, 1,279,000

GERMANY
Official Name: Federal Republic of Germany
Population: 81,710,000
Area: 137,822 sq. mi. (356,955 sq. km.)
Pop. Density: 593/sq. mi. (229/sq. km.)
Capital: Berlin (designated), 3,433,695, and
  Bonn (de facto), 292,234

GHANA
Official Name: Republic of Ghana
Population: 17,210,000
Area: 92,098 sq. mi. (238,533 sq. km.)
Pop. Density: 187/sq. mi. (72/sq. km.)
Capital: Accra, 949,113

GREECE
Official Name: Hellenic Republic
Population: 10,475,000
Area: 50,949 sq. mi. (131,957 sq. km.)
Pop. Density: 206/sq. mi. (79/sq. km.)
Capital: Athens (Athínai), 748,110

GREENLAND
Official Name: Greenland
Population: 57,000
Area: 840,004 sq. mi. (2,175,600 sq. km.)
Pop. Density: 0.1/sq. mi. (0.03/sq. km.)
Capital: Godthåb (Nuuk), 12,217

GRENADA
Official Name: Grenada
Population: 92,000
Area: 133 sq. mi. (344 sq. km.)
Pop. Density: 692/sq. mi. (267/sq. km.)
Capital: St. George's, 4,439

GUATEMALA
Official Name: Republic of Guatemala
Population: 10,420,000
Area: 42,042 sq. mi. (108,889 sq. km.)
Pop. Density: 248/sq. mi. (96/sq. km.)
Capital: Guatemala, 1,057,210

GUINEA
Official Name: Republic of Guinea
Population: 6,469,000
Area: 94,926 sq. mi. (245,857 sq. km.)
Pop. Density: 68/sq. mi. (26/sq. km.)
Capital: Conakry, 800,000

GUINEA-BISSAU
Official Name: Republic of Guinea-Bissau
Population: 1,111,000
Area: 13,948 sq. mi. (36,125 sq. km.)
Pop. Density: 80/sq. mi. (31/sq. km.)
Capital: Bissau, 125,000

GUYANA
Official Name: Co-operative Republic of
  Guyana
Population: 726,000
Area: 83,000 sq. mi. (214,969 sq. km.)
Pop. Density: 8.7/sq. mi. (3.4/sq. km.)
Capital: Georgetown, 78,500

HAITI
Official Name: Republic of Haiti
Population: 7,069,000
Area: 10,714 sq. mi. (27,750 sq. km.)
Pop. Density: 660/sq. mi. (255/sq. km.)
Capital: Port-au-Prince, 797,000

HONDURAS
Official Name: Republic of Honduras
Population: 5,822,000
Area: 43,277 sq. mi. (112,088 sq. km.)
Pop. Density: 135/sq. mi. (52/sq. km.)
Capital: Tegucigalpa, 576,661

HUNGARY
Official Name: Republic of Hungary
Population: 10,270,000
Area: 35,919 sq. mi. (93,030 sq. km.)
Pop. Density: 286/sq. mi. (110/sq. km.)
Capital: Budapest, 2,016,774

Countries and Flags
continued

IRELAND
Official Name: Ireland
Population: 3,546,000
Area: 27,137 sq. mi. (70,285 sq. km.)
Pop. Density: 131/sq. mi. (50/sq. km.)
Capital: Dublin (Baile Átha Cliath), 502,749

KAZAKHSTAN
Official Name: Republic of Kazakhstan
Population: 17,025,000
Area: 1,049,156 sq. mi. (2,717,300 sq. km.)
Pop. Density: 16/sq. mi. (6.3/sq. km.)
Capital: Alma-Ata (Almaty), 1,156,200, and
Akmola (future), 286,000

ICELAND
Official Name: Republic of Iceland
Population: 265,000
Area: 39,769 sq. mi. (103,000 sq. km.)
Pop. Density: 6.7/sq. mi. (2.6/sq. km.)
Capital: Reykjavik, 100,850

ISRAEL
Official Name: State of Israel
Population: 5,059,000
Area: 8,019 sq. mi. (20,770 sq. km.)
Pop. Density: 631/sq. mi. (244/sq. km.)
Capital: Jerusalem (Yerushalayim), 524,500

KENYA
Official Name: Republic of Kenya
Population: 28,380,000
Area: 224,961 sq. mi. (582,646 sq. km.)
Pop. Density: 126/sq. mi. (49/sq. km.)
Capital: Nairobi, 1,505,000

INDIA
Official Name: Republic of India
Population: 909,150,000
Area: 1,237,062 sq. mi. (3,203,975 sq. km.)
Pop. Density: 735/sq. mi. (284/sq. km.)
Capital: New Delhi, 301,297

ITALY
Official Name: Italian Republic
Population: 57,330,000
Area: 116,324 sq. mi. (301,277 sq. km.)
Pop. Density: 493/sq. mi. (190/sq. km.)
Capital: Rome (Roma), 2,693,383

KIRIBATI
Official Name: Republic of Kiribati
Population: 79,000
Area: 313 sq. mi. (811 sq. km.)
Pop. Density: 252/sq. mi. (97/sq. km.)
Capital: Bairiki, 2,226

INDONESIA
Official Name: Republic of Indonesia
Population: 193,680,000
Area: 752,410 sq. mi. (1,948,732 sq. km.)
Pop. Density: 257/sq. mi. (99/sq. km.)
Capital: Jakarta, 8,227,746

JAMAICA
Official Name: Jamaica
Population: 2,568,000
Area: 4,244 sq. mi. (10,991 sq. km.)
Pop. Density: 605/sq. mi. (234/sq. km.)
Capital: Kingston, 587,798

KOREA, NORTH
Official Name: Democratic People's Republic
of Korea
Population: 23,265,000
Area: 46,540 sq. mi. (120,538 sq. km.)
Pop. Density: 500/sq. mi. (193/sq. km.)
Capital: P'yŏngyang, 2,355,000

IRAN
Official Name: Islamic Republic of Iran
Population: 63,810,000
Area: 632,457 sq. mi. (1,638,057 sq. km.)
Pop. Density: 101/sq. mi. (39/sq. km.)
Capital: Tehrān, 6,042,584

JAPAN
Official Name: Japan
Population: 125,360,000
Area: 145,870 sq. mi. (377,801 sq. km.)
Pop. Density: 859/sq. mi. (332/sq. km.)
Capital: Tōkyō, 8,163,573

KOREA, SOUTH
Official Name: Republic of Korea
Population: 44,655,000
Area: 38,230 sq. mi. (99,016 sq. km.)
Pop. Density: 1,168/sq. mi. (451/sq. km.)
Capital: Seoul (Sŏul), 10,627,790

IRAQ
Official Name: Republic of Iraq
Population: 20,250,000
Area: 169,235 sq. mi. (438,317 sq. km.)
Pop. Density: 120/sq. mi. (46/sq. km.)
Capital: Baghdād, 3,841,268

JORDAN
Official Name: Hashemite Kingdom of
Jordan
Population: 4,028,000
Area: 35,135 sq. mi. (91,000 sq. km.)
Pop. Density: 115/sq. mi. (44/sq. km.)
Capital: 'Ammān, 936,300

KUWAIT
Official Name: State of Kuwait
Population: 1,866,000
Area: 6,880 sq. mi. (17,818 sq. km.)
Pop. Density: 271/sq. mi. (105/sq. km.)
Capital: Kuwait (Al Kuwayt), 44,335

KYRGYZSTAN
Official Name: Kyrgyz Republic
Population: 4,541,000
Area: 76,641 sq. mi. (198,500 sq. km.)
Pop. Density: 59/sq. mi. (23/sq. km.)
Capital: Bishkek, 631,300

LIBYA
Official Name: Socialist People's Libyan
  Arab Jamahiriya
Population: 5,148,000
Area: 679,362 sq. mi. (1,759,540 sq. km.)
Pop. Density: 7.6/sq. mi. (2.9/sq. km.)
Capital: Tripoli (Ṭarābulus), 591,062

MALAWI
Official Name: Republic of Malawi
Population: 8,984,000
Area: 45,747 sq. mi. (118,484 sq. km.)
Pop. Density: 196/sq. mi. (76/sq. km.)
Capital: Lilongwe, 223,318

LAOS
Official Name: Lao People's Democratic
  Republic
Population: 4,768,000
Area: 91,429 sq. mi. (236,800 sq. km.)
Pop. Density: 52/sq. mi. (20/sq. km.)
Capital: Viangchan (Vientiane), 377,409

LIECHTENSTEIN
Official Name: Principality of Liechtenstein
Population: 30,000
Area: 62 sq. mi. (160 sq. km.)
Pop. Density: 484/sq. mi. (188/sq. km.)
Capital: Vaduz, 4,887

MALAYSIA
Official Name: Malaysia
Population: 19,505,000
Area: 127,320 sq. mi. (329,758 sq. km.)
Pop. Density: 153/sq. mi. (59/sq. km.)
Capital: Kuala Lumpur, 919,610

LATVIA
Official Name: Republic of Latvia
Population: 2,532,000
Area: 24,595 sq. mi. (63,700 sq. km.)
Pop. Density: 103/sq. mi. (40/sq. km.)
Capital: Rīga, 910,200

LITHUANIA
Official Name: Republic of Lithuania
Population: 3,757,000
Area: 25,212 sq. mi. (65,300 sq. km.)
Pop. Density: 149/sq. mi. (58/sq. km.)
Capital: Vilnius, 596,900

MALDIVES
Official Name: Republic of Maldives
Population: 251,000
Area: 115 sq. mi. (298 sq. km.)
Pop. Density: 2,183/sq. mi. (842/sq. km.)
Capital: Male', 55,130

LEBANON
Official Name: Republic of Lebanon
Population: 3,660,000
Area: 4,015 sq. mi. (10,400 sq. km.)
Pop. Density: 912/sq. mi. (352/sq. km.)
Capital: Beirut (Bayrūt), 509,000

LUXEMBOURG
Official Name: Grand Duchy of Luxembourg
Population: 396,000
Area: 998 sq. mi. (2,586 sq. km.)
Pop. Density: 397/sq. mi. (153/sq. km.)
Capital: Luxembourg, 75,377

MALI
Official Name: Republic of Mali
Population: 9,585,000
Area: 482,077 sq. mi. (1,248,574 sq. km.)
Pop. Density: 20/sq. mi. (7.7/sq. km.)
Capital: Bamako, 658,275

LESOTHO
Official Name: Kingdom of Lesotho
Population: 1,967,000
Area: 11,720 sq. mi. (30,355 sq. km.)
Pop. Density: 168/sq. mi. (65/sq. km.)
Capital: Maseru, 109,382

MACEDONIA
Official Name: Republic of Macedonia
Population: 2,102,000
Area: 9,928 sq. mi. (25,713 sq. km.)
Pop. Density: 212/sq. mi. (82/sq. km.)
Capital: Skopje, 444,900

MALTA
Official Name: Republic of Malta
Population: 368,000
Area: 122 sq. mi. (316 sq. km.)
Pop. Density: 3,016/sq. mi. (1,165/sq. km.)
Capital: Valletta, 9,199

LIBERIA
Official Name: Republic of Liberia
Population: 2,771,000
Area: 38,250 sq. mi. (99,067 sq. km.)
Pop. Density: 72/sq. mi. (28/sq. km.)
Capital: Monrovia, 465,000

MADAGASCAR
Official Name: Republic of Madagascar
Population: 13,645,000
Area: 226,658 sq. mi. (587,041 sq. km.)
Pop. Density: 60/sq. mi. (23/sq. km.)
Capital: Antananarivo, 1,250,000

MARSHALL ISLANDS
Official Name: Republic of the Marshall
  Islands
Population: 55,000
Area: 70 sq. mi. (181 sq. km.)
Pop. Density: 786/sq. mi. (304/sq. km.)
Capital: Majuro (island)

Countries and Flags
continued

MONACO
Official Name: Principality of Monaco
Population: 31,000
Area: 0.7 sq. mi. (1.9 sq. km.)
Pop. Density: 44,286/sq. mi. (16,316/sq. km.)
Capital: Monaco, 31,000

NAURU
Official Name: Republic of Nauru
Population: 10,000
Area: 8.1 sq. mi. (21 sq. km.)
Pop. Density: 1,235/sq. mi. (476/sq. km.)
Capital: Yaren District

MAURITANIA
Official Name: Islamic Republic of
Mauritania
Population: 2,228,000
Area: 395,956 sq. mi. (1,025,520 sq. km.)
Pop. Density: 5.6/sq. mi. (2.2/sq. km.)
Capital: Nouakchott, 285,000

MONGOLIA
Official Name: Mongolia
Population: 2,462,000
Area: 604,829 sq. mi. (1,566,500 sq. km.)
Pop. Density: 4.1/sq. mi. (1.6/sq. km.)
Capital: Ulan Bator (Ulaanbaatar), 575,000

NEPAL
Official Name: Kingdom of Nepal
Population: 21,295,000
Area: 56,827 sq. mi. (147,181 sq. km.)
Pop. Density: 375/sq. mi. (145/sq. km.)
Capital: Kathmandu, 421,258

MAURITIUS
Official Name: Republic of Mauritius
Population: 1,121,000
Area: 788 sq. mi. (2,040 sq. km.)
Pop. Density: 1,423/sq. mi. (550/sq. km.)
Capital: Port Louis, 141,870

MOROCCO
Official Name: Kingdom of Morocco
Population: 26,890,000
Area: 172,414 sq. mi. (446,550 sq. km.)
Pop. Density: 156/sq. mi. (60/sq. km.)
Capital: Rabat, 518,616

NETHERLANDS
Official Name: Kingdom of the Netherlands
Population: 15,425,000
Area: 16,164 sq. mi. (41,864 sq. km.)
Pop. Density: 954/sq. mi. (368/sq. km.)
Capital: Amsterdam (designated), 713,407,
and 's-Gravenhage (The Hague) (seat of
government), 445,287

MEXICO
Official Name: United Mexican States
Population: 93,860,000
Area: 759,534 sq. mi. (1,967,183 sq. km.)
Pop. Density: 124/sq. mi. (48/sq. km.)
Capital: Mexico City (Ciudad de México),
8,235,744

MOZAMBIQUE
Official Name: Republic of Mozambique
Population: 17,860,000
Area: 308,642 sq. mi. (799,380 sq. km.)
Pop. Density: 58/sq. mi. (22/sq. km.)
Capital: Maputo, 1,069,727

NEW ZEALAND
Official Name: New Zealand
Population: 3,558,000
Area: 104,454 sq. mi. (270,534 sq. km.)
Pop. Density: 34/sq. mi. (13/sq. km.)
Capital: Wellington, 150,301

MICRONESIA, FEDERATED STATES OF
Official Name: Federated States of
Micronesia
Population: 122,000
Area: 271 sq. mi. (702 sq. km.)
Pop. Density: 450/sq. mi. (174/sq. km.)
Capital: Kolonia (de facto), 6,169, and
Paliker (future)

MYANMAR
Official Name: Union of Myanmar
Population: 44,675,000
Area: 261,228 sq. mi. (676,577 sq. km.)
Pop. Density: 171/sq. mi. (66/sq. km.)
Capital: Yangon (Rangoon), 2,513,023

NICARAGUA
Official Name: Republic of Nicaragua
Population: 4,438,000
Area: 50,054 sq. mi. (129,640 sq. km.)
Pop. Density: 89/sq. mi. (34/sq. km.)
Capital: Managua, 682,000

MOLDOVA
Official Name: Republic of Moldova
Population: 4,377,000
Area: 13,012 sq. mi. (33,700 sq. km.)
Pop. Density: 336/sq. mi. (130/sq. km.)
Capital: Chişinău (Kishinev), 676,700

NAMIBIA
Official Name: Republic of Namibia
Population: 1,623,000
Area: 318,253 sq. mi. (824,272 sq. km.)
Pop. Density: 5.1/sq. mi. (2.0/sq. km.)
Capital: Windhoek, 114,500

NIGER
Official Name: Republic of Niger
Population: 9,125,000
Area: 489,191 sq. mi. (1,267,000 sq. km.)
Pop. Density: 19/sq. mi. (7.2/sq. km.)
Capital: Niamey, 392,165

NIGERIA
Official Name: Federal Republic of Nigeria
Population: 97,300,000
Area: 356,669 sq. mi. (923,768 sq. km.)
Pop. Density: 273/sq. mi. (105/sq. km.)
Capital: Lagos (de facto),1,213,000, and
  Abuja (designated), 250,000

PALAU
Official Name: Republic of Palau
Population: 17,000
Area: 196 sq. mi. (508 sq. km.)
Pop. Density: 87/sq. mi. (33/sq. km.)
Capital: Koror (de facto), 9,018, and
  Melekeok (future)

POLAND
Official Name: Republic of Poland
Population: 38,730,000
Area: 121,196 sq. mi. (313,895 sq. km.)
Pop. Density: 320/sq. mi. (123/sq. km.)
Capital: Warsaw (Warszawa), 1,644,500

NIUE
Official Name: Niue
Population: 1,900
Area: 100 sq. mi. (259 sq. km.)
Pop. Density: 19/sq. mi. (7.3/sq. km.)
Capital: Alofi, 706

PANAMA
Official Name: Republic of Panama
Population: 2,654,000
Area: 29,157 sq. mi. (75,517 sq. km.)
Pop. Density: 91/sq. mi. (35/sq. km.)
Capital: Panamá, 411,549

PORTUGAL
Official Name: Portuguese Republic
Population: 9,907,000
Area: 35,516 sq. mi. (91,985 sq. km.)
Pop. Density: 279/sq. mi. (108/sq. km.)
Capital: Lisbon (Lisboa), 807,167

NORTHERN MARIANA ISLANDS
Official Name: Commonwealth of the
  Northern Mariana Islands
Population: 51,000
Area: 184 sq. mi. (477 sq. km.)
Pop. Density: 277/sq. mi. (107/sq. km.)
Capital: Saipan (island)

PAPUA NEW GUINEA
Official Name: Independent State of Papua
  New Guinea
Population: 4,057,000
Area: 178,704 sq. mi. (462,840 sq. km.)
Pop. Density: 23/sq. mi. (8.8/sq. km.)
Capital: Port Moresby, 193,242

PUERTO RICO
Official Name: Commonwealth of Puerto Rico
Population: 3,625,000
Area: 3,515 sq. mi. (9,104 sq. km.)
Pop. Density: 1,031/sq. mi. (398/sq. km.)
Capital: San Juan, 426,832

NORWAY
Official Name: Kingdom of Norway
Population: 4,339,000
Area: 149,412 sq. mi. (386,975 sq. km.)
Pop. Density: 29/sq. mi. (11/sq. km.)
Capital: Oslo, 470,204

PARAGUAY
Official Name: Republic of Paraguay
Population: 4,400,000
Area: 157,048 sq. mi. (406,752 sq. km.)
Pop. Density: 28/sq. mi. (11/sq. km.)
Capital: Asunción, 502,426

QATAR
Official Name: State of Qatar
Population: 519,000
Area: 4,412 sq. mi. (11,427 sq. km.)
Pop. Density: 118/sq. mi. (45/sq. km.)
Capital: Ad Dawḥah (Doha), 217,294

OMAN
Official Name: Sultanate of Oman
Population: 2,089,000
Area: 82,030 sq. mi. (212,457 sq. km.)
Pop. Density: 25/sq. mi. (9.8/sq. km.)
Capital: Masqat (Muscat), 30,000

PERU
Official Name: Republic of Peru
Population: 23,095,000
Area: 496,225 sq. mi. (1,285,216 sq. km.)
Pop. Density: 47/sq. mi. (18/sq. km.)
Capital: Lima, 371,122

ROMANIA
Official Name: Romania
Population: 22,745,000
Area: 91,699 sq. mi. (237,500 sq. km.)
Pop. Density: 248/sq. mi. (96/sq. km.)
Capital: Bucharest (Bucureşti), 2,064,474

PAKISTAN
Official Name: Islamic Republic of Pakistan
Population: 129,630,000
Area: 339,732 sq. mi. (879,902 sq. km.)
Pop. Density: 382/sq. mi. (147/sq. km.)
Capital: Islāmābād, 204,364

PHILIPPINES
Official Name: Republic of the Philippines
Population: 67,910,000
Area: 115,831 sq. mi. (300,000 sq. km.)
Pop. Density: 586/sq. mi. (226/sq. km.)
Capital: Manila, 1,598,918

RUSSIA
Official Name: Russian Federation
Population: 150,500,000
Area: 6,592,849 sq. mi. (17,075,400 sq. km.)
Pop. Density: 23/sq. mi. (8.8/sq. km.)
Capital: Moscow (Moskva), 8,801,500

Countries and Flags
continued

SAO TOME AND PRINCIPE
Official Name: Democratic Republic of Sao Tome and Principe
Population: 127,000
Area: 372 sq. mi. (964 sq. km.)
Pop. Density: 341/sq. mi. (132/sq. km.)
Capital: São Tomé, 5,245

SLOVAKIA
Official Name: Slovak Republic
Population: 5,353,000
Area: 18,933 sq. mi. (49,035 sq. km.)
Pop. Density: 283/sq. mi. (109/sq. km.)
Capital: Bratislava, 441,453

RWANDA
Official Name: Republic of Rwanda
Population: 7,343,000
Area: 10,169 sq. mi. (26,338 sq. km.)
Pop. Density: 722/sq. mi. (279/sq. km.)
Capital: Kigali, 232,733

SAUDI ARABIA
Official Name: Kingdom of Saudi Arabia
Population: 18,190,000
Area: 830,000 sq. mi. (2,149,690 sq. km.)
Pop. Density: 22/sq. mi. (8.5/sq. km.)
Capital: Riyadh (Ar Riyād), 1,250,000

SLOVENIA
Official Name: Republic of Slovenia
Population: 1,993,000
Area: 7,820 sq. mi. (20,253 sq. km.)
Pop. Density: 255/sq. mi. (98/sq. km.)
Capital: Ljubljana, 233,200

ST. KITTS AND NEVIS
Official Name: Federation of St. Kitts and Nevis
Population: 42,000
Area: 104 sq. mi. (269 sq. km.)
Pop. Density: 404/sq. mi. (156/sq. km.)
Capital: Basseterre, 14,725

SENEGAL
Official Name: Republic of Senegal
Population: 8,862,000
Area: 75,951 sq. mi. (196,712 sq. km.)
Pop. Density: 117/sq. mi. (45/sq. km.)
Capital: Dakar, 1,490,450

SOLOMON ISLANDS
Official Name: Solomon Islands
Population: 393,000
Area: 10,954 sq. mi. (28,370 sq. km.)
Pop. Density: 36/sq. mi. (14/sq. km.)
Capital: Honiara, 30,413

ST. LUCIA
Official Name: St. Lucia
Population: 138,000
Area: 238 sq. mi. (616 sq. km.)
Pop. Density: 580/sq. mi. (224/sq. km.)
Capital: Castries, 11,147

SEYCHELLES
Official Name: Republic of Seychelles
Population: 75,000
Area: 175 sq. mi. (453 sq. km.)
Pop. Density: 429/sq. mi. (166/sq. km.)
Capital: Victoria, 23,000

SOMALIA
Official Name: Somalia
Population: 7,187,000
Area: 246,201 sq. mi. (637,657 sq. km.)
Pop. Density: 29/sq. mi. (11/sq. km.)
Capital: Mogadishu (Muqdisho), 600,000

ST. VINCENT AND THE GRENADINES
Official Name: St. Vincent and the Grenadines
Population: 110,000
Area: 150 sq. mi. (388 sq. km.)
Pop. Density: 733/sq. mi. (284/sq. km.)
Capital: Kingstown, 15,466

SIERRA LEONE
Official Name: Republic of Sierra Leone
Population: 4,690,000
Area: 27,925 sq. mi. (72,325 sq. km.)
Pop. Density: 168/sq. mi. (65/sq. km.)
Capital: Freetown, 469,776

SOUTH AFRICA
Official Name: Republic of South Africa
Population: 44,500,000
Area: 471,010 sq. mi. (1,219,909 sq. km.)
Pop. Density: 94/sq. mi. (36/sq. km.)
Capital: Pretoria (administrative), 525,583, Cape Town (legislative), 854,616, and Bloemfontein (judicial), 126,867

SAN MARINO
Official Name: Republic of San Marino
Population: 24,000
Area: 24 sq. mi. (61 sq. km.)
Pop. Density: 1,000/sq. mi. (393/sq. km.)
Capital: San Marino, 2,794

SINGAPORE
Official Name: Republic of Singapore
Population: 2,921,000
Area: 246 sq. mi. (636 sq. km.)
Pop. Density: 11,874/sq. mi. (4,593/sq. km.)
Capital: Singapore, 2,921,000

SPAIN
Official Name: Kingdom of Spain
Population: 39,260,000
Area: 194,885 sq. mi. (504,750 sq. km.)
Pop. Density: 201/sq. mi. (78/sq. km.)
Capital: Madrid, 3,102,846

SRI LANKA
Official Name: Democratic Socialist Republic
of Sri Lanka
Population: 18,240,000
Area: 24,962 sq. mi. (64,652 sq. km.)
Pop. Density: 731/sq. mi. (282/sq. km.)
Capital: Colombo (designated), 612,000, and
Sri Jayawardenepura (seat of government),
108,000

SUDAN
Official Name: Republic of the Sudan
Population: 25,840,000
Area: 967,500 sq. mi. (2,505,813 sq. km.)
Pop. Density: 27/sq. mi. (10/sq. km.)
Capital: Khartoum (Al Kharṭum), 473,597

SURINAME
Official Name: Republic of Suriname
Population: 426,000
Area: 63,251 sq. mi. (163,820 sq. km.)
Pop. Density: 6.7/sq. mi. (2.6/sq. km.)
Capital: Paramaribo, 241,000

SWAZILAND
Official Name: Kingdom of Swaziland
Population: 889,000
Area: 6,704 sq. mi. (17,364 sq. km.)
Pop. Density: 133/sq. mi. (51/sq. km.)
Capital: Mbabane (administrative), 38,290,
and Lobamba (legislative)

SWEDEN
Official Name: Kingdom of Sweden
Population: 8,981,000
Area: 173,732 sq. mi. (449,964 sq. km.)
Pop. Density: 52/sq. mi. (20/sq. km.)
Capital: Stockholm, 674,452

SWITZERLAND
Official Name: Swiss Confederation
Population: 7,244,000
Area: 15,943 sq. mi. (41,293 sq. km.)
Pop. Density: 454/sq. mi. (175/sq. km.)
Capital: Bern (Berne), 136,338

SYRIA
Official Name: Syrian Arab Republic
Population: 14,100,000
Area: 71,498 sq. mi. (185,180 sq. km.)
Pop. Density: 197/sq. mi. (76/sq. km.)
Capital: Damascus (Dimashq), 1,549,932

TAIWAN
Official Name: Republic of China
Population: 21,150,000
Area: 13,900 sq. mi. (36,002 sq. km.)
Pop. Density: 1,522/sq. mi. (587/sq. km.)
Capital: T'aipei, 2,706,453

TAJIKISTAN
Official Name: Republic of Tajikistan
Population: 6,073,000
Area: 55,251 sq. mi. (143,100 sq. km.)
Pop. Density: 110/sq. mi. (42/sq. km.)
Capital: Dushanbe, 582,400

TANZANIA
Official Name: United Republic of Tanzania
Population: 28,350,000
Area: 341,217 sq. mi. (883,749 sq. km.)
Pop. Density: 83/sq. mi. (32/sq. km.)
Capital: Dar es Salaam (de facto), 1,096,000,
and Dodoma (legislative), 85,000

THAILAND
Official Name: Kingdom of Thailand
Population: 59,870,000
Area: 198,115 sq. mi. (513,115 sq. km.)
Pop. Density: 302/sq. mi. (117/sq. km.)
Capital: Bangkok (Krung Thep), 5,620,591

TOGO
Official Name: Republic of Togo
Population: 4,332,000
Area: 21,925 sq. mi. (56,785 sq. km.)
Pop. Density: 198/sq. mi. (76/sq. km.)
Capital: Lomé, 500,000

TONGA
Official Name: Kingdom of Tonga
Population: 110,000
Area: 288 sq. mi. (747 sq. km.)
Pop. Density: 382/sq. mi. (147/sq. km.)
Capital: Nuku'alofa, 21,265

TRINIDAD AND TOBAGO
Official Name: Republic of Trinidad and
Tobago
Population: 1,281,000
Area: 1,980 sq. mi. (5,128 sq. km.)
Pop. Density: 647/sq. mi. (250/sq. km.)
Capital: Port of Spain, 50,878

TUNISIA
Official Name: Republic of Tunisia
Population: 8,806,000
Area: 63,170 sq. mi. (163,610 sq. km.)
Pop. Density: 139/sq. mi. (54/sq. km.)
Capital: Tunis, 596,654

TURKEY
Official Name: Republic of Turkey
Population: 62,030,000
Area: 300,948 sq. mi. (779,452 sq. km.)
Pop. Density: 206/sq. mi. (80/sq. km.)
Capital: Ankara, 2,559,471

TURKMENISTAN
Official Name: Turkmenistan
Population: 4,035,000
Area: 188,456 sq. mi. (488,100 sq. km.)
Pop. Density: 21/sq. mi. (8.3/sq. km.)
Capital: Ashkhabad, 412,200

TUVALU
Official Name: Tuvalu
Population: 10,000
Area: 10 sq. mi. (26 sq. km.)
Pop. Density: 1,000/sq. mi. (385/sq. km.)
Capital: Funafuti, 2,191

Countries
and Flags
continued

URUGUAY
Official Name: Oriental Republic of Uruguay
Population: 3,317,000
Area: 68,500 sq. mi. (177,414 sq. km.)
Pop. Density: 48/sq. mi. (19/sq. km.)
Capital: Montevideo, 1,251,647

WESTERN SAMOA
Official Name: Independent State of Western
Samoa
Population: 172,000
Area: 1,093 sq. mi. (2,831 sq. km.)
Pop. Density: 157/sq. mi. (61/sq. km.)
Capital: Apia, 34,126

UGANDA
Official Name: Republic of Uganda
Population: 18,270,000
Area: 93,104 sq. mi. (241,139 sq. km.)
Pop. Density: 196/sq. mi. (76/sq. km.)
Capital: Kampala, 773,463

UZBEKISTAN
Official Name: Republic of Uzbekistan
Population: 22,860,000
Area: 172,742 sq. mi. (447,400 sq. km.)
Pop. Density: 132/sq. mi. (51/sq. km.)
Capital: Tashkent, 2,113,300

YEMEN
Official Name: Republic of Yemen
Population: 12,910,000
Area: 203,850 sq. mi. (527,968 sq. km.)
Pop. Density: 63/sq. mi. (24/sq. km.)
Capital: Sana, 427,150

UKRAINE
Official Name: Ukraine
Population: 52,140,000
Area: 233,090 sq. mi. (603,700 sq. km.)
Pop. Density: 224/sq. mi. (86/sq. km.)
Capital: Kiev (Kyyiv), 2,635,000

VANUATU
Official Name: Republic of Vanuatu
Population: 161,000
Area: 4,707 sq. mi. (12,190 sq. km.)
Pop. Density: 34/sq. mi. (13/sq. km.)
Capital: Port Vila, 18,905

YUGOSLAVIA
Official Name: Socialist Federal Republic of
Yugoslavia
Population: 10,765,000
Area: 39,449 sq. mi. (102,173 sq. km.)
Pop. Density: 273/sq. mi. (105/sq. km.)
Capital: Belgrade (Beograd), 1,136,786

UNITED ARAB EMIRATES
Official Name: United Arab Emirates
Population: 2,855,000
Area: 32,278 sq. mi. (83,600 sq. km.)
Pop. Density: 88/sq. mi. (34/sq. km.)
Capital: Abū Ẓaby (Abu Dhabi), 242,975

VATICAN CITY
Official Name: State of the Vatican City
Population: 1,000
Area: 0.2 sq. mi. (0.4 sq. km.)
Pop. Density: 5,000/sq. mi. (2,500/sq. km.)
Capital: Vatican City, 1,000

ZAIRE
Official Name: Republic of Zaire
Population: 43,365,000
Area: 905,355 sq. mi. (2,344,858 sq. km.)
Pop. Density: 48/sq. mi. (18/sq. km.)
Capital: Kinshasa, 3,000,000

UNITED KINGDOM
Official Name: United Kingdom of Great
Britain and Northern Ireland
Population: 58,430,000
Area: 94,249 sq. mi. (244,101 sq. km.)
Pop. Density: 620/sq. mi. (239/sq. km.)
Capital: London, 6,574,009

VENEZUELA
Official Name: Republic of Venezuela
Population: 21,395,000
Area: 352,145 sq. mi. (912,050 sq. km.)
Pop. Density: 61/sq. mi. (23/sq. km.)
Capital: Caracas, 1,822,465

ZAMBIA
Official Name: Republic of the Zambia
Population: 8,809,000
Area: 290,587 sq. mi. (752,618 sq. km.)
Pop. Density: 30/sq. mi. (12/sq. km.)
Capital: Lusaka, 982,362

UNITED STATES
Official Name: United States of America
Population: 262,530,000
Area: 3,787,425 sq. mi. (9,809,431 sq. km.)
Pop. Density: 69/sq. mi. (27/sq. km.)
Capital: Washington, D.C., 606,900

VIETNAM
Official Name: Socialist Republic of Vietnam
Population: 73,760,000
Area: 127,428 sq. mi. (330,036 sq. km.)
Pop. Density: 579/sq. mi. (223/sq. km.)
Capital: Ha Noi, 905,939

ZIMBABWE
Official Name: Republic of Zimbabwe
Population: 11,075,000
Area: 150,872 sq. mi. (390,757 sq. km.)
Pop. Density: 73/sq. mi. (28/sq. km.)
Capital: Harare (Salisbury), 681,000

Map Symbols

In a very real sense, the whole map is a symbol, representing the world or a part of it. It is a reduced representation of the earth; each of the world's features–cities rivers, etc.–is represented on the map by a symbol. Map symbols may take the form of points, such as dots or squares (often used for cities, capital cities, or points of interest), or lines (roads, railroads, rivers). Symbols may also occupy an area, showing extent of coverage (terrain, forests, deserts). They seldom look like the feature they represent and therefore must be identified and interpreted. For instance, the maps in this atlas define political units by colored tints. Neither the colors nor the boundary lines are actually found on the surface of the earth, but because countries and states are such important political components of the world, strong symbols are used to represent them. On the maps in this atlas the surface configuration of the earth is represented by hill-shading, which gives the three-dimensional impression of landforms. This terrain representation conveys a realistic and readily visualized impression of the surface. A complete legend to the right provides a key to the other symbols on the maps in this atlas.

In this atlas a "local-name" policy generally was used for naming cities and towns and all local topographic and water features. However, for a few major cities the Anglicized name was preferred and the local name given in parentheses, for instance, Moscow (Moskva), Vienna (Wien), Prague (Praha). In countries where more than one official language is used, a name is in the dominant local language. The generic parts of local names for topographic and water features are self-explanatory in many cases because of the associated map symbols or type styles.

Cultural Features

Political Boundaries

International

Secondary: State, Provincial, etc. (Second order political unit)

Disputed de jure

Cities, Towns and Villages
(Note: On maps at 1:45,000,000 and smaller the town symbols do not follow the specific population classification shown below.)

PARIS — 1,000,000 and over

Milwaukee — 250,000 to 1,000,000

Huntsville — 100,000 to 250,000

Bloomington — 25,000 to 100,000

New Meadows — 0 to 25,000

BUDAPEST — National Capitals

Springfield — Secondary Capitals

Other Cultural Features

Research Stations

Ruins

Transportation

Primary Roads

Secondary Roads

Railroads

Topographic Features

Nev. Sajama 21,463 — Peaks
Elevations are given in feet

Water Features

Lakes and Reservoirs

Fresh Water

Fresh Water: Intermittent

Salt Water

Other Water Features

Rivers

Rivers: Intermittent

Reefs

Ice Shelf

ARCTIC OCEAN

75°

GREENLAND
(Den.)

Baffin
Bay

ICELAND

ALASKA
(U.S.)

Dawson

60°

Anchorage

Reykjavik

NORTH

Hudson
Bay

UNITED
KINGD...

Juneau

C A N A D A

Edmonton

IRELAND

45°

Winnipeg

Vancouver

NEWFOUNDLAND

Seattle

Montréal

St. John's

AMERICA

Detroit

Ottawa

San Francisco

Chicago

New York

UNITED STATES

Washington

AZORES
(Port.)

PORTUGAL

30°

Los Angeles

Atlanta

GIBRALTAR
(U.K.)

Tropic of Cancer

Houston

ATLANTIC

CANARY ISLANDS
(Sp.)

MIDWAY IS.
(U.S.)

New Orleans

MAR...

MEXICO

Gulf of Mexico

BAHAMAS

W. SAHARA

Havana

MAURITANIA

HAWAIIAN ISLANDS
(U.S.)

Mexico City

Veracruz

CUBA

15°

DOM. REP.

HAITI

PUERTO RICO (U.S.)

BELIZE

SENEGAL

PACIFIC

GUAT.

JAMAICA

GUADELOUPE (Fr.)

CAPE VERDE

Dakar

HOND.

Caribbean

MARTINIQUE (Fr.)

GAMBIA

EL SAL.

NIC.

Sea

BARBADOS

GUINEA-BISSAU

GUINEA

COSTA
RICA

TRINIDAD AND TOBAGO

SIERRA LEONE

PALMYRA
(U.S.)

PANAMA

Caracas

GUYANA

VENEZUELA

Georgetown

LIBERIA

0°

Equator

Bogotá

SURINAME

FRENCH GUIANA

COLOMBIA

KIRIBATI

GALAPAGOS ISLANDS
(Ecua.)

Quito

Belém

ECUADOR

Manaus

Fortaleza

SOUTH

G

MARQUESAS IS.
(Fr.)

BRAZIL

Recife

PERU

AMERICA

OCEAN

Lima

Salvador

WESTERN
SAMOA

OCEAN

15°

La Paz

AMERICAN
SAMOA

BOLIVIA

Brasília

TONGA

COOK
ISLANDS
(N.Z.)

TAHITI

Sucre

FRENCH POLYNESIA

Rio de Janeiro

Tropic of Capricorn

PARAGUAY

São Paulo

Antofagasta

EASTER ISLAND
(Chile)

30°

ARGENTINA

Valparaíso

URUGUAY

ARCH. DE JUAN
FERNÁNDEZ
(Chile)

Santiago

Buenos
Aires

Montevideo

CHATHAM IS.
(N.Z.)

45°

FALKLAND IS.
(U.K.)

SOUTH GEORGIA
(U.K.)

Punta Arenas

TIERRA DEL FUEGO

SOUTH SANDWICH IS.
(U.K.)

SOUTH ORKNEY IS.
(U.K.)

60°

SOUTH SHETLAND IS.
(U.K.)

Weddell

Scale 1:100,000,000; one inch to 1578 miles
Robinson Projection

Sea

Antarctic Circle

75°

0	400	800	1200	1600	2000 Miles
0	600	1200	1800	2400	3000 Kilometers

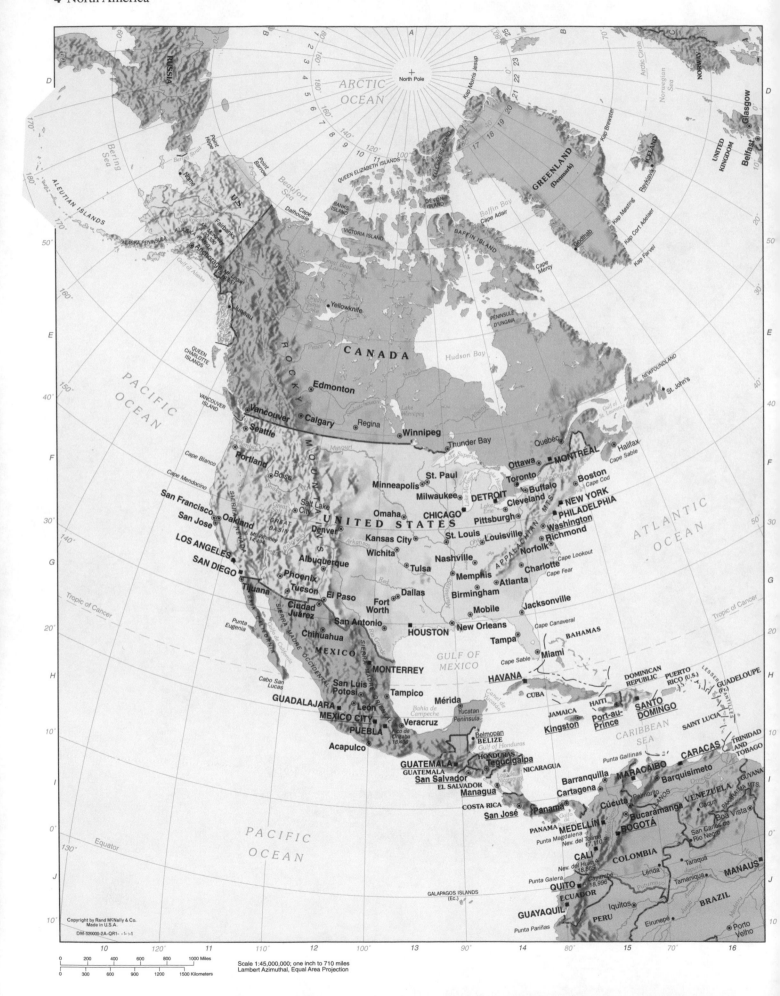

Scale 1:45,000,000; one inch to 710 miles
Lambert Azimuthal, Equal Area Projection

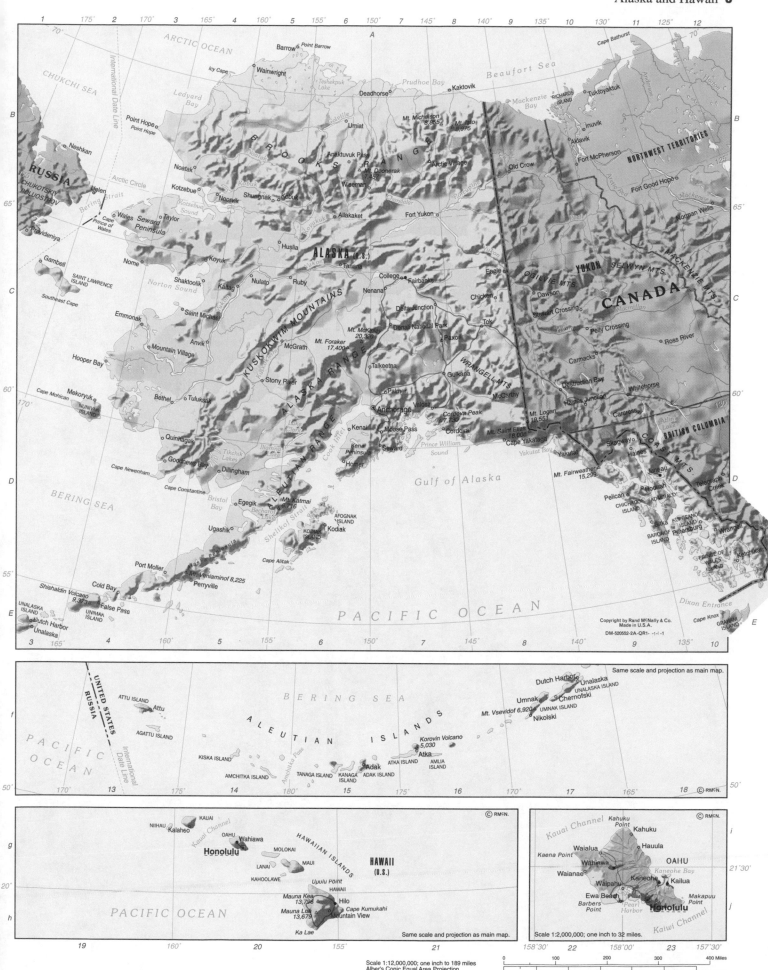

Copyright by Rand McNally & Co.
Made in U.S.A.
DM-520552-2A-QR1- -1-/-1

Same scale and projection as main map.

© RMcN.

© RMcN.

Same scale and projection as main map.

Scale 1:2,000,000; one inch to 32 miles.

Scale 1:12,000,000; one inch to 189 miles
Alber's Conic Equal Area Projection

Scale 1:16,000,000; one inch to 252 miles
Lambert Conformal Conic Projection

| 0 | 100 | 200 | 300 | 400 | 500 Miles |
| 0 | 200 | 400 | 600 | 800 Kilometers |

Scale 1:12,000,000; one inch to 189 miles
Alber's Conic Equal Area Projection

0   100   200   300   400 Miles

0   100   200   300   400   500   600 Kilometers

ATLANTIC

OCEAN

A T L A N T I C   O C E A N

GULF
OF
MEXICO

BAHAMAS

Tropic of Cancer

NORTH CAROLINA

SOUTH CAROLINA

GEORGIA

FLORIDA

ALABAMA

TENNESSEE

MISS.

Virginia Beach
Norfolk
Portsmouth
Suffolk
Emporia
Roanoke Rapids
Rocky Mount
Greenville
Washington
New Bern
Morehead City
Kinston
Goldsboro
Jacksonville
Wilmington
Carolina Beach
Cape Fear
Myrtle Beach
Conway
Georgetown
Charleston
Beaufort
Walterboro
Savannah
Brunswick
St. Marys
Jacksonville
Jacksonville Beach
St. Augustine
Daytona Beach
Titusville
Cape Canaveral
Cocoa
New Smyrna Beach
Merritt Island
Melbourne
Vero Beach
Fort Pierce
West Palm Beach
Fort Lauderdale
Hollywood
Hialeah
Miami
Homestead
Key Largo
Key West
FLORIDA KEYS
East Cape
Cape Sable
Everglades City
Naples
Fort Myers
Port Charlotte
Sarasota
St. Petersburg
Tampa
Tampa Bay
Clearwater
Tarpon Springs
Lakeland
Orlando
Ocala
Gainesville
Lake Okeechobee
Belle Glade
Cross City
Cedar Key
Homosassa
Perry
Tallahassee
Thomasville
Bainbridge
Port Saint Joe
Panama City
Cape San Blas
Crestview
Pensacola
Mobile
Pascagoula
Dothan
Ozark
Troy
Evergreen
Greenville
Brewton
Montgomery
Selma
Tuscaloosa
Birmingham
Jasper
Cullman
Homewood
Sylacauga
Gadsden
Anniston
Auburn
Phenix City
Columbus
La Grange
Carrollton
Rome
Dalton
Chattanooga
Atlanta
Marietta
Americus
Albany
Cordele
Tifton
Moultrie
Valdosta
Waycross
Hazlehurst
Douglas
Statesboro
Dublin
Milledgeville
Macon
Griffin
Athens
Gainesville
Greensboro
Augusta
Aiken
Columbia
Sumter
Florence
Lake City
Lumberton
Fayetteville
Raleigh
Durham
Chapel Hill
Greensboro
Winston-Salem
High Point
Lexington
Salisbury
Charlotte
Gastonia
Rock Hill
Greenwood
Greenville
Spartanburg
Anderson
Hendersonville
Asheville
Morganton
Hickory
Mt. Mitchell 6,684
Easley
Clarks Hill Lake
Madison
Decatur
Florence
Russellville
Huntsville
Tullahoma
Nashville
Clarksville
Hopkinsville
Columbia
Lewisburg
Lawrenceburg
Corinth
Tupelo
Columbus
Meridian
West Point
Thomasville
Jackson
Dyersburg
Humboldt
Union City
Paris
Clinton
Oak Ridge
Knoxville
Mt. Oglethorpe 3,288
Red Bank
Johnson City
Bristol
Kingsport
Mount Airy
Black Mountain 6,684
BLUE RIDGE
Martinsville
Danville
Roanoke
Bluefield
Middlesboro
Glasgow
Green
Murray

Pamlico Sound
Albemarle Sound
Cape Hatteras
HATTERAS ISLAND
Manteo
Edenton
Elizabeth City
Cape Lookout
Roanoke
Cape Fear
Pee Dee
Great Pee Dee
Santee
Savannah
Altamaha
Ocmulgee
Oconee
Flint
Chattahoochee
Apalachicola
Alabama
Tombigbee
Tennessee
Cumberland
Kentucky Lake
Lake Barkley
Dale Hollow Lake
John H. Kerr Reservoir
Clarks Hill Lake
Suwannee

LITTLE ABACO ISLAND
GREAT ABACO
Marsh Harbour
GRAND BAHAMA
Freeport
NEW PROVIDENCE
Nassau
Nicolls Town
ANDROS ISLAND
Kemps Bay
ELEUTHERA
Governor's Harbour
Arthur's Town
CAT ISLAND
George Town
LONG ISLAND
SAN SALVADOR
Straits of Florida
Florida

Scale 1:8,000,000; one inch to 126 miles
Lambert Conformal Conic Projection

0   50   100   150   200   250 Miles
0   100   200   300   400 Kilometers

Copyright by Rand McNally & Co.
Made in U.S.A.
DM-500269-2A-QIR1 - 4-1-1

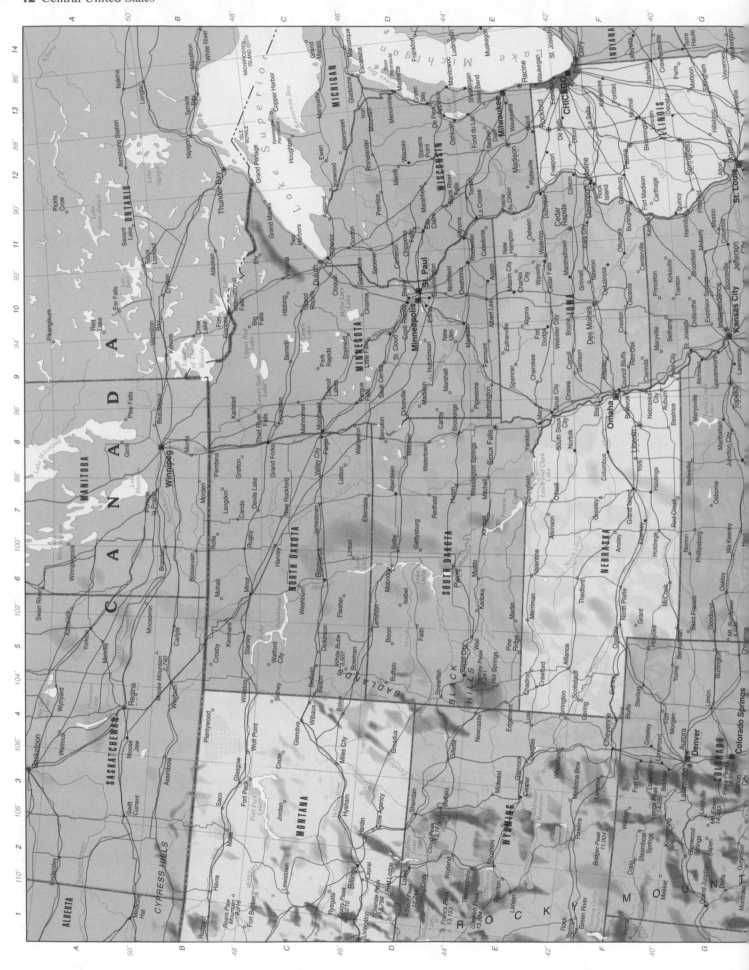

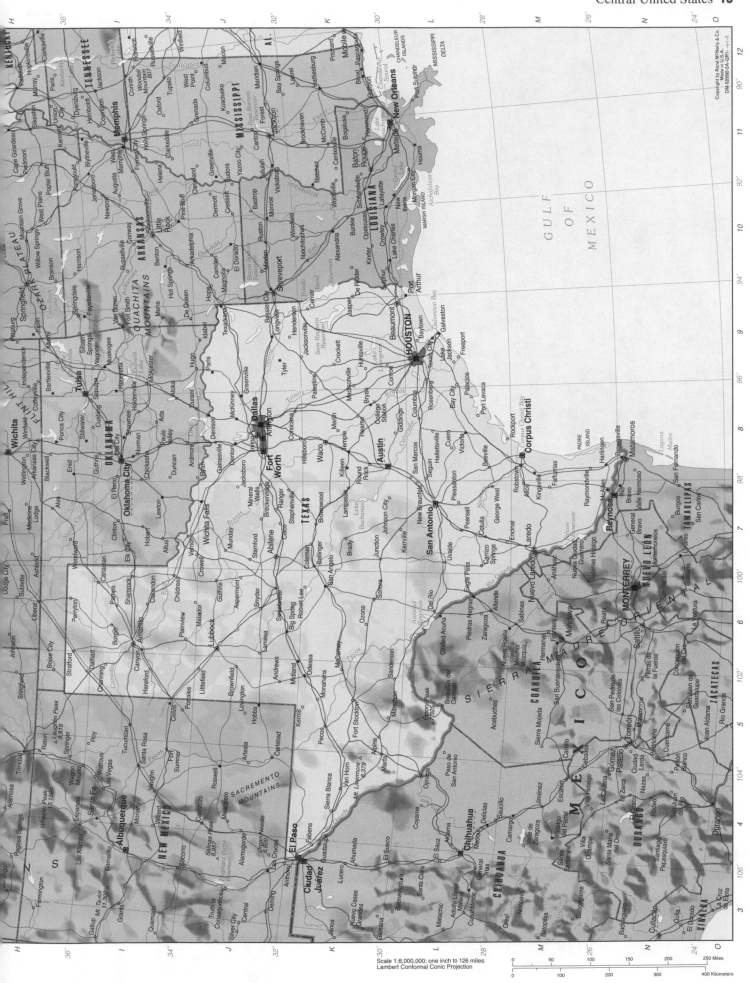

Scale 1:8,000,000; one inch to 126 miles
Lambert Conformal Conic Projection

0   50   100   150   200   250 Miles

0   100   200   300   400 Kilometers

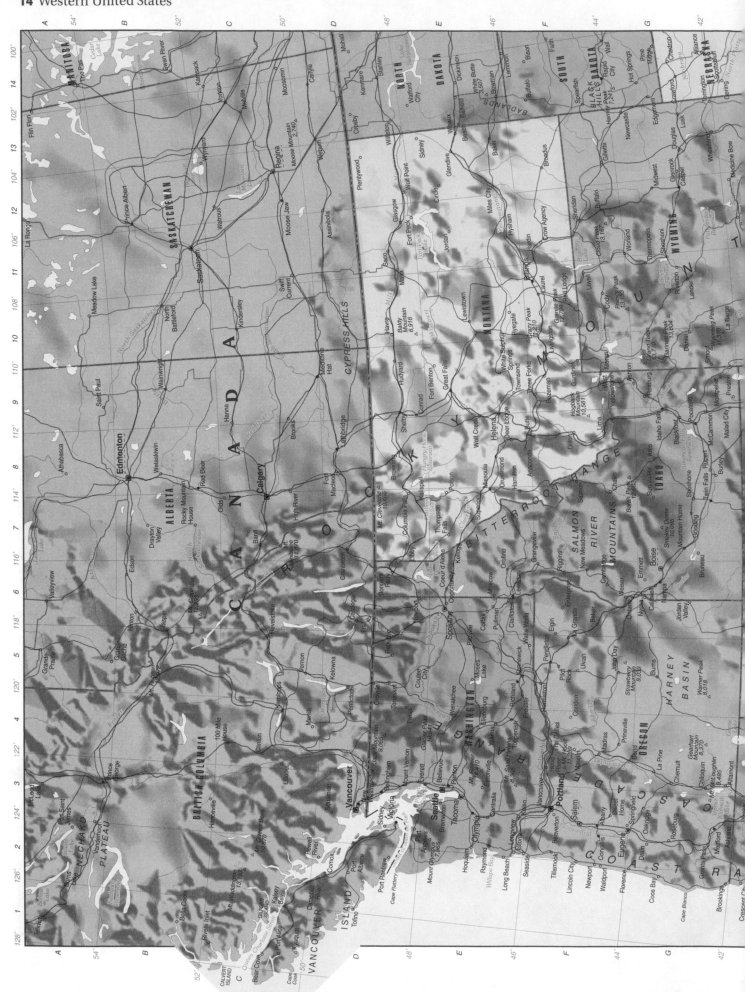

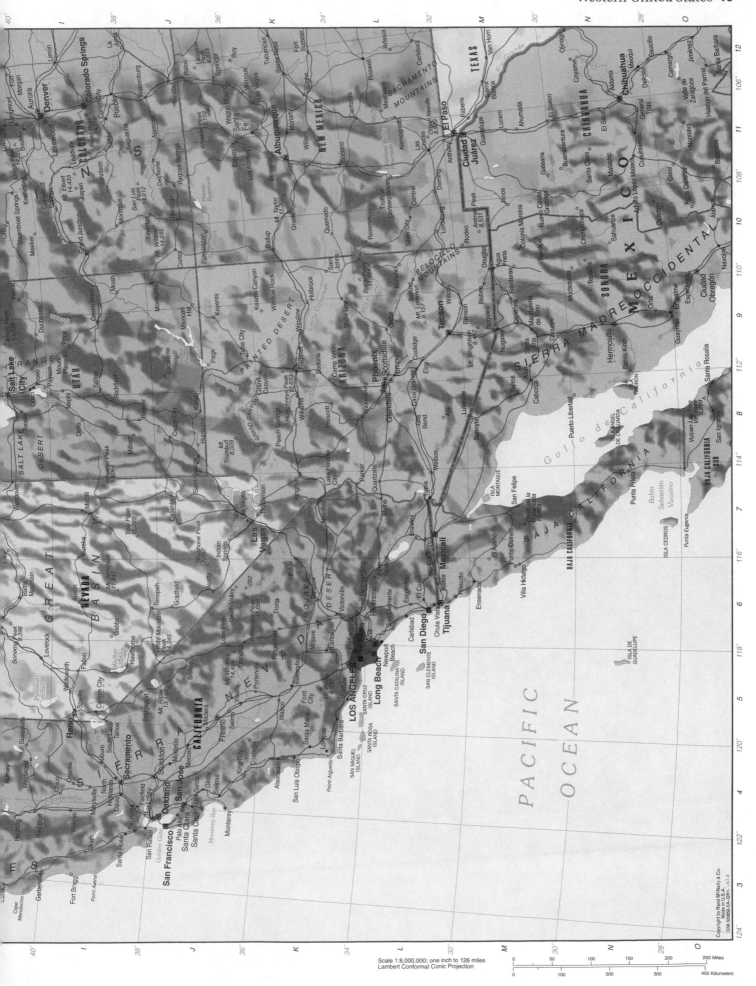

Scale 1:8,000,000; one inch to 126 miles
Lambert Conformal Conic Projection

0   50   100   150   200   250 Miles

0   100   200   300   400 Kilometers

ATLANTIC OCEAN

CARIBBEAN SEA

WEST INDIES

GREATER ANTILLES

LESSER ANTILLES

Tropic of Cancer

BAHAMAS

CUBA

JAMAICA

HAITI
HISPANIOLA
DOMINICAN REPUBLIC

SANTO DOMINGO

PUERTO RICO (U.S.)

VENEZUELA

COLOMBIA

PANAMA

GUYANA

SURINAME

BRAZIL

FLORIDA

VIRGINIA

NORTH CAROLINA

SOUTH CAROLINA

BERMUDA (U.K.)

Scale 1:16,000,000; one inch to 252 miles
Lambert Conformal Conic Projection

0   100   200   300   400   500 Miles
0   200   400   600   800 Kilometers

PACIFIC OCEAN

Golfo de California

BAJA CALIFORNIA

BAJA CALIFORNIA SUR

ARIZONA

NEW MEXICO

SONORA

CHIHUAHUA

COAH

DURANGO

SINALOA

ZACATECA

NAYARIT

JALISCO

Tropic of Cancer

Tijuana
Mexicali
Ensenada
Tucson
El Paso
Ciudad Juárez
Chihuahua
Hermosillo
Guaymas
Ciudad Obregón
Los Mochis
Culiacán
Durango
Mazatlán
Tepic
GUADALAJARA
COLIMA

0   50   100   150   200   250
0   100   200   300   400

GULF OF MEXICO

Scale 1:8,000,000; one inch to 126 miles
Lambert Conformal Conic Projection

Scale 1:45,000,000; one inch to 710 miles
Lambert Azimuthal, Equal Area Projection

Scale 1:16,000,000; one inch to 252 miles
Lambert Conformal Conic Projection

PACIFIC OCEAN

NICARAGUA

COSTA RICA

PANAMA

COLOMBIA

ECUADOR

PERU

VENEZUELA

BOLIVIA

ARGENTINA

AMAZONAS

ACRE

ROND

GALAPAGOS ISLANDS
(ARCHIPIELAGO DE COLÓN)
(Ecuador)

SAN CRISTOBAL

ISLA DEL COCO
(Costa Rica)

ISLA DE MALPELO
(Colombia)

NETHERLANDS ANTILLES

ARUBA
(Neth.)

CURAÇAO   BONAIRE

Oranjestad   Willemstad

ISLA DE MARGARITA

Equator

CORDILLERA OCCIDENTAL

CORDILLERA ORIENTAL

CORDILLERA DEL CONDOR

CORD. ULTRAORIENTAL

CORDILLERA ORIENTAL

CORDILLERA DE HUANZO

CORDILLERA OCCIDENTAL

CORD. REAL

ALTIPLANO

SIERRA PARIMA

SIERRA DE CURUPIRA

ANDES

Lago de Maracaibo

Lago Titicaca

Lago Poopó

Cities and places:

San José, Puntarenas, Puerto Limón, Alajuela, San Isidro, Davis, Volcán Irazú 11,260, Cerro Chirripó 12,530, Volcán Barú 11,401, STMO, Colón, Panamá, Chorrera, Aguadulce, Santiago, Chitre, Puerto Armuelles, Punta Burica, ISLA DE COIBA, Punta Mariato, ISLA DEL REY, Punta Mala, Riosucio, Punta Marzo, Chigorodó

Barranquilla, Cartagena, Santa Marta, Ciénaga, Sabanalarga, Soledad, Valledupar, Turbaco, Plato, El Banco, San Jacinto, Sincelejo, Corozal, Sahagún, Lorica, Cereté, Montería, San Marcos, Caucasia, Turbo, MARACAIBO, Maicao, Riohacha, Coro, Puerto Cabello, Cabimas, Machiques, Barquisimeto, Valencia, Maracay, CARACAS, Petare, Guarenas, Guacara, Carora, Acarigua, Barinas, San Fernando, Mérida, Trujillo, Valera, Guanare, Cúcuta, San Cristóbal, Pamplona, Bucaramanga, Floridablanca, Barrancabermeja, Yarumal, Bello, Puerto Berrío, Itagüí, MEDELLÍN, Envigado, La Dorada, Honda, Duitama, Sogamoso, Tunja, Yopal, Manizales, Pereira, Armenia, Cartago, Tuluá, Buga, Espinal, Ibagué, BOGOTÁ, Villavicencio, CALI, Palmira, Neiva, San Martín, Popayán, Pitalito, Florencia, Tumaco, Pasto, Ipiales, Esmeraldas

Ciudad Guayana, Ciudad Bolívar, El Tigre, Guanipa, Valle de la Pascua, Calabozo, Puerto Ayacucho, San Carlos de Río Negro, Lérida, Taraqua, Tefé, Tamaniquá, Leticia, Iquitos, Pucallpa, Cruzeiro do Sul, Eirunepé, Rio Branco, Porto, Ariquemes, Guajará-Mirim, Puerto Maldonado, Puerto Heath, Trinidad

Quito, Cotopaxi 19,347, Chone, Manta, Portoviejo, Jipijapa, Vinces, Babahoyo, Milagro, Ambato, Riobamba, Chimborazo 20,702, Vol. Sangay 17,165, GUAYAQUIL, Cañar, Cuenca, Machala, Pasaje, Tumbes, Loja, Cayambe 18,996

Talara, Sullana, Piura, Castilla, Sechura, Jaén, Chiclayo, Lambayeque, Pacasmayo, Chocope, Trujillo, Cajamarca, Chachapoyas, Moyobamba, Yurimaguas, Chimbote, Nev. Huascarán 22,133, Huaraz, Huánuco, Tingo María, Nevado Yerupaja 21,765, Cerro de Pasco, Huarmey, Pativilca, Huacho, Punta Lachay, La Oroya, Tarma, Callao, Lima, Vitarte, Chosica, Huancayo, Huancavelica, Ayacucho, Cusco, Abancay, Machupicchu, Nevado Ausangate 20,945, Chincha Alta, Pisco, Ica, Ayaviri, Nazca, Nevado Coropuna 20,686, Juliaca, Puno, Nevado Chachani 19,931, Arequipa, Volcán Misti 19,101, Nev. Illampu 21,066, LA PAZ, Camaná, Moliendo, Moquegua, Ilo, Volcán Tutupaca 19,898, Tacna, Arica, Nev. Illimani 20,741, Cochabamba, Oruro, Santa Cruz de la Sierra, Sucre, Pisagua, Iquique, Pozo Almonte, Nev. Sajama 21,463, Potosí, Tocopilla, Chuquicamata, Calama, Cerro Licancabur 19,409

Scale: 0 100 200 300 400 500 Miles
0 200 400 600 800 Kilometers

ATLANTIC OCEAN

TRINIDAD AND TOBAGO
of Spain
Fernando
RINIDAD

Morawhanna
Marlborough
Charity
Suddie
Parika
Bartica
New Amsterdam
Nieuw
Nickerie
Groningen
Georgetown
Enmore
Paramaribo
Nieuw Amsterdam
Iracoubo
Sinnamary
Albina
Kourou
Saint-Laurent-du-Maroni
Cayenne
Saint-Élie
Guisanbourg
Quanary
Saûl

GUYANA
Mount Roraima 9,432
Kwakoegron
Brokopondo
Stuwmeer
SURINAME
Juliana-Top 4,035
**FRENCH
GUIANA**
Cabo Cacipore

Lethem
KANUKU
MTS.
KAMOA
MTS.
ACARAI MTS.
TUMUC-HUMAC MOUNTAINS
AMAPÁ
ILHA DE MARACÁ
Cabo Norte

a Vista

ILHA BAILIQUE
ILHA DO CURUÁ
ILHA JANAUCU
Macapá
ILHA CAVIANA DE FORA
ILHA MEXIANA

Oriximiná
Faro
ILHA
GRANDE
DO GURUPÁ
Cabo Maguari
Equator

ILHA DE
MARAJÓ
Soure
Baía de Marajó
Bragança
Capanema
Carutapera
Belém
Abaetetuba
Castanhal
São
Luís
Parnaíba
Camocim
Itapipoca

Novo
Aripuanã
MANAUS
Itacoatiara
Maués
Santarém
Braves
Portel
Cametá
Pindaré Mirim
Bacabal
Coroatá
Codó
Piripiri
Sobral
Canindé
Pacajus
Fortaleza
Maracanaú
Manacapuru
Altamira
Tucuruí
Caxias
Campo
Maior
CEARÁ
Crateús
Quixadá
Mossoró

Itaituba
Represa de
Tucuruí
Pedreiras
Timon
Teresina
Jaguaribe
Igatu
Caió
RÍO GRANDE DO NORTE
Natal
Cabo de São Roque

Conceiçao
PARÁ
SERRA DOS CARAJÁS
Marabá
Imperatriz
MARANHÃO
São João dos
Patos
Floriano
Picos
Oeiras
Crato
Juazeiro
do Norte
Patos
Guarabira
PARAÍBA
**João
Pessoa**
Campina
Grande
Itabaiana

Nazaré
Tocantinópolis
PIAUÍ
Salgueiro
Serra Talhada
PERNAMBUCO
Aroverde
RECIFE
Caruaru
Olinda

Araguaína
Carolina
Balsas
Represa Boa
Esperança
Petrolina
Juazeiro
Paulo Afonso
Palmares
Garanhuns
Palmeira dos
Indios
ALAGOAS
Maceió

Conceição
da Araguaia
SERRA
DO ESPIGÃO
CHAPADA DAS MANGABEIRAS
SERRA DO PENITENTE
Curuá
Senhor do
Bonfim
Jacobina
Arapiraca
Penedo
SERGIPE

Alta Floresta
SERRA DOS APIACÁS
B R A Z I L
Palmas
Porto Nacional
TOCANTINS
Gurupi
SERRA DO URUÇUÍ
Irecê
Aracaju

Vilhena
SERRA DO NORTE
MATO GROSSO
SERRA FORMOSA
SERRA DO RONCADOR
Barreiras
Ibotirama
BAHÍA
Itaberaba
Esplanada
Alagoinhas
**Feira de
Santana**

Diamantino
**PLANALTO
DO MATO
GROSSO**
Porangatu
Santana
Bom Jesus
da Lapa
Camaçari
SALVADOR
Valença

SERRA DOS PARECIS
Guanambi
Brumado
Jequié
Ipiaú
Itabuna
Ilhéus

Cáceres
Cuiabá
Juçara
Inhumas
BRASÍLIA
DISTRITO FEDERAL
Formosa
Januária
Vitória da
Conquista
Itapetinga
Canavieiras
Belmonte

Jaciara
Barra do Garças
Iporá
Caiapônia
Luziânia
Unaí
São
Francisco
Salinas
Pedra Azul
Almenara
Itamaraju

Rondonópolis
Goiânia
GOIÁS
Pontalina
Paracatu
Montes Claros
Bocaiúva
Pirapora
Itaobim
Ponta da Baleia

Mineiros
Jataí
Pires do
Rio
João
Pinheiro
Patos de
Minas
**MINAS
GERAIS**
Teófilo Otoni
Nanuque

Corumbá
Coxim
Rio Verde
de Mato Grosso
Harumá
Itumbiara
Araguari
Curvelo
Governador
Valadares
São Mateus

**MATO GROSSO
DO SUL**
Camapuã
Paranaíba
Campina
Verde
Uberlândia
Sete Lagoas
Ipatinga
Linhares

Puerto Bahía
Negra
Miranda
Aquidauana
Três Lagoas
Frutal
Uberaba
Araxá
**BELO
HORIZONTE**
Vitória
Vila Velha

Dourados
Campo Grande
**São José do
Rio Preto**
Campinas
França
Lavras
São João
del Rei
Ponte Nova
Cachoeiro de Itapemirim

SA. DE MARACAJU
Bela Vista
Araçatuba
SÃO PAULO
Araraquara
Pocos de Caldas
Volta
Redonda
Juiz de Fora
RIO DE JANEIRO
Cabo de São Tomé

Presidente
Prudente
Marília
Assis
Lins
São Carlos
Três Rios
Nova
Friburgo
Campos

Pedro Juan
Caballero
Ponta Porã
Bauru
Piracicaba
Campinas
Itaquari
Nova Iguaçu
Niterói

ARAGUAY
Tupã
São José dos Campos
Sorocaba
SÃO PAULO
Santo André
Taubaté
Santos
RIO DE JANEIRO
São Vicente
Tropic of Capricorn

O BOREAL

Copyright by Rand McNally & Co.
Made in U.S.A.
DM-549100-2A-QR1- -1-1-1

Scale 1:16,000,000; one inch to 252 miles
Lambert Azimuthal, Equal Area Projection

North Pole

ARCTIC OCEAN

ATLANTIC OCEAN

IRELAND

UNITED KINGDOM

LONDON

PARIS

FRANCE

PORTUGAL

SPAIN

ALGIERS

Tunis

MEDITERRANEAN SEA

LIBYA

Tripoli

Banghazi

ALEXANDRIA

CAIRO

EGYPT

LIBYAN DESERT

SUDAN

Khartoum

ETHIOPIA

ADDIS ABABA

KENYA

NAIROBI

TANZANIA

Mombasa

DAR ES SALAAM

MOZAMBIQUE

COMOROS

MADAGASCAR

NORWAY

SWEDEN

FINLAND

NORTH SEA

GERMANY

POLAND

BELARUS

EST.

LITH.

LAT.

SAINT PETERSBURG (LENINGRAD)

Arkhangel'sk

MOSCOW (MOSKVA)

NIZHNIY NOVGOROD (GORKY)

KIEV (KYIV)

UKRAINE

KHARKIV

Saratov

PERM

KAZAN'

URAL MOUNTAINS

Serov

Surgut

RUSSIA

SIBERIA

Norilsk

Yakut

VERKHOYANSKIY KHREBET

EAST SIBERIAN

LAPTEV SEA

NEW SIBERIAN ISLANDS

BARENTS SEA

NOVAYA ZEMLYA

KARA SEA

SEVERNAYA ZEMLYA

ZEMLYA FRANTSA

SVALBARD

ROMANIA

BULG.

HUNG.

GREECE

ISTANBUL

TURKEY

ANKARA

CYPRUS

LEBANON

SYRIA

DAMASCUS

ISRAEL

JORDAN

BLACK SEA

ODESA

ROSTOV-NA-DONU

VOLGOGRAD

ASTRAKHAN'

Makhachkala

GEORGIA

TBILISI

ARMENIA

YEREVAN

AZERBAIJAN

BAKU

CASPIAN SEA

CASPIAN DEPRESSION

Atyrau

Aktau

SAMARA

YEKATERINBURG (SVERDLOVSK)

CHELYABINSK

OMSK

Akmola

Karaganda

Semipalatinsk

NOVOSIBIRSK

Tomsk

Bratsk

Irkutsk

Ulan-Ude

SAYAN KHREBET

ALTAI MTS

Ulan Bator

MONGOLIA

GOBI DESERT

ÜRÜMQI

BEIJING

TAIYUAN

TIANJ

JIN

ZHENGZHOU

XI'AN

QIN LING

LANZHOU

CHINA

WUHAN

CHENGDU

CHONGQING

KUNMING

GUANGZHO

Aktyubinsk

KAZAKHSTAN

Kyzyl-Orda

Aral Sea

Lake Balkash

Bishkek

ALMA-ATA

KYRGYZSTAN

TIEN SHAN

TASHKENT

UZBEKISTAN

TURKMENISTAN

Ashkhabad

MASHHAD

TEHRAN

Esfahan

IRAN

TAJIKISTAN

Dushanbe

Herat

AFGHANISTAN

KABOL

TARIM BASIN

ALTUN SHAN

KUNLUN SHAN

K2 (Qogir Feng) 28,250

PLATEAU OF TIBET

Lhasa

Mt. Everest 29,028

Kathmandu

NEPAL

Thimphu

BHUTAN

BANGLA-DESH

DHAKA

CHITTAGONG

MYANMAR (BURMA)

Mandalay

LAOS

Viangchan

Ha Noi

Hai Phong

Da Na

VIE

THANH HO CH (SAIGO)

KÁBOL

Islamabad

LAHORE

FAISALABAD

PAKISTAN

DELHI

JAIPUR

New Delhi

KÁNPUR

GREAT INDIAN DESERT

HIMALAYA

Ganges

Brahmaputra

AHMADĀBĀD

INDIA

NĀGPUR

CALCUTTA

HYDERABAD

BOMBAY

PUNE

WESTERN GHATS

EASTERN GHATS

DECCAN

BANGALORE

MADRAS

BAY OF BENGAL

Pagoda Point

ANDAMAN ISLANDS (India)

NICOBAR ISLANDS (India)

THAILAND

BANGKOK

CAMBODIA

Phnum Penh

Gulf of Thailand

Mui Ca Mau

MALAY PENINSULA

Str. of Malacca

MALAYSIA

Kuala Lumpur

SINGAPORE

SUMATRA

PALEMBANG

JAKARTA

PLATEAU OF IRAN

ZAGROS MTS

BAGHDAD

IRAQ

Tabriz

Kuwait

KUWAIT

Shiraz

Bandar-e 'Abbas

Persian Gulf

Ad Dammam

RIYADH

BAHRAIN

QATAR

Ad Dawhah

Abū Zaby

U.A.E.

Gulf of Oman

Ra's al Hadd

OMAN

SAUDI ARABIA

JIDDAH

Red Sea

AR RUB' AL KHĀLĪ

YEMEN

Sana

Aden (Adan)

Gulf of Aden

Ra's Fartak

SOCOTRA (SUQUTRA) (Yem.)

Gees Gwardafuy

DJIBOUTI

SOMALIA

ERITREA

Asmera

ETHIOPIAN PLATEAU

KARĀCHI

ARABIAN SEA

LAKSHADWEEP (India)

MALDIVES

Male'

Cape Comorin

SRI LANKA

Colombo

Sri Jayawardenepura

Dondra Head

SEYCHELLES

INDIAN OCEAN

UGANDA

Blue Nile

Nile

AL HIJAZ

SINAI

AMMAN

Tropic of Cancer

Equator

Arctic Circle

Mogadishu

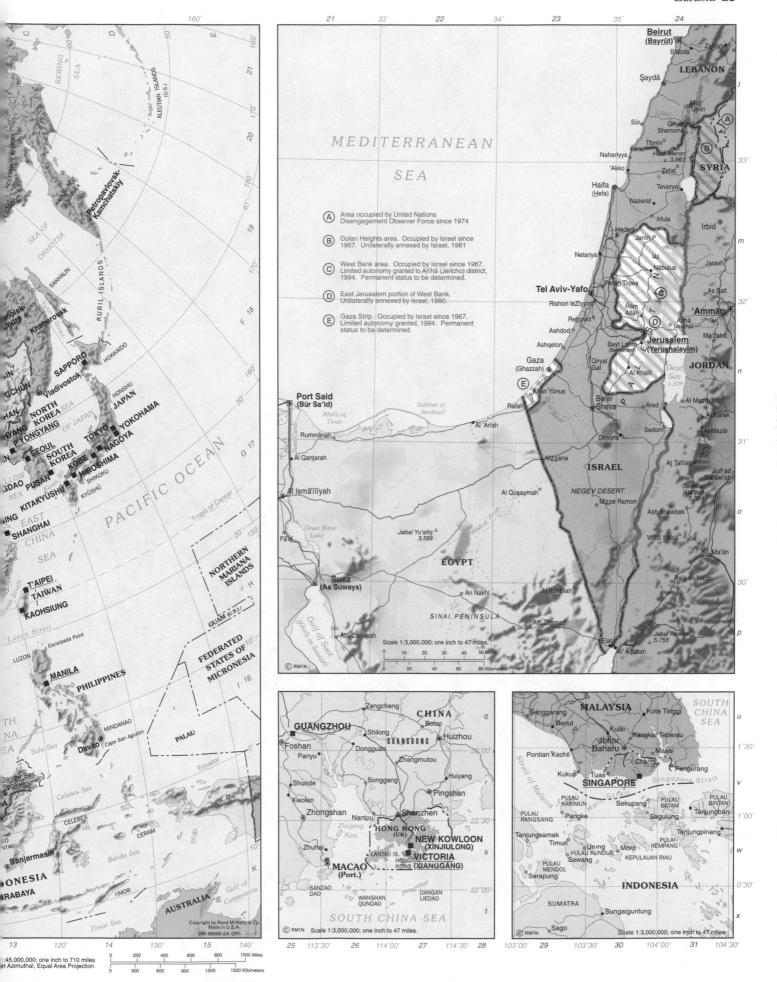

ICELAND
Reykjavik
Akureyri
Rifstangi
Fontur
Horn
Djúpivogur
Stokksnes

ATLANTIC OCEAN

NORWEGIAN SEA

Arctic Circle

FAEROE IS. (Den.)
Tórshavn

SHETLAND ISLANDS
Lerwick

ORKNEY ISLANDS
Duncansby Head
Wick
Moray Firth

HEBRIDES

SCOTLAND
Glasgow
Aberdeen
Dundee
Edinburgh
Newcastle upon Tyne
GRAMPIAN MTS
Kinnaird Head
Forth of Forth
CHEVIOT HILLS

NORWAY
Trondheim
Bergen
Stavanger
Lindesnes
Oslo
Sognafjorden

SWEDEN
Umeå
Örnsköldsvik
Östersund
Härnösand
Sarna
Gävle
Uppsala
Stockholm
Norrköping
Linköping
Visby
GOTLAND
Göteborg
ÖLAND

DENMARK
Ålborg
Copenhagen (København)
Malmö
Kattegat
Grenen
Skagerrak

Turku
Tampere

BALTIC SEA
Klaipéda
Liepa
Kolkas Rags
Kaliningrad

IRELAND
Bloody Foreland
Achill Head
Galway
Dublin
Limerick
Cork
Loop Head
Mizen Head
Irish Sea

NORTHERN IRELAND
Belfast

UNITED KINGDOM
Liverpool
Manchester
Leicester
Kingston upon Hull
Birmingham
WALES
Cardiff
ENGLAND
LONDON
Southampton
Portsmouth
Plymouth
St. George's Channel
Hartland Point
Land's End
Lizard Point

NORTH SEA

NETHERLANDS
Amsterdam
The Hague ('s-Gravenhage)
Rotterdam

BELGIUM
Brussels

GERMANY
Bremerhaven
Kiel
Rostock
Bremen
Hannover
Berlin
Magdeburg
Essen
Bonn
Leipzig
Dresden
Frankfurt
Mainz
Nürnberg
Stuttgart
MUNICH (MÜNCHEN)
Hamburg

POLAND
Gdańsk
Szczecin
Toruń
Poznań
Łódź
Wrocław
Katowice
WARSAW (WARSZAWA)

BORNHOLM (Den.)

English Channel
CHANNEL IS. (U.K.)
Cherbourg
Le Havre
Rouen
Lille
Reims

FRANCE
Brest
Pointe du Raz
Rennes
Nantes
PARIS
Orléans
Tours
Limoges
Dijon
Strasbourg
Mulhouse
LUX. Luxembourg
Lyon
Bordeaux
Bay of Biscay
Pointe de la Coubre
MASSIF CENTRAL
Nîmes
Avignon
Marseille
Toulon
Golfe du Lion

SWITZERLAND
Zürich
Bern
Lausanne
Genève
Mont Blanc

LIECH.
AUSTRIA
VIENNA (WIEN)
Graz
Innsbruck

CZECH REPUBLIC
PRAGUE (PRAHA)
Plzeň
Ostrava
SUDETES

SLOVAKIA
Bratislava
Kraków

HUNGARY
BUDAPEST
Győr
Debrecen
Szeged

PORTUGAL
Cabo Ortegal
La Coruña
Cabo de Finisterre
Vigo
Porto
Cabo Mondego
Coimbra
LISBON (Lisboa)
Cabo da Roca
Cabo de São Vicente
Faro

SPAIN
Gijón
Oviedo
Santander
Bilbao
Donostia
Logroño
Valladolid
Salamanca
Zaragoza
MADRID
Toledo
Badajoz
Córdoba
Sevilla
Granada
Murcia
Alacant
València
BARCELONA
Tarragona
ANDORRA
PYRENEES
Toulouse
SIERRA MORENA
SISTEMAS BÉTICOS
Albacete
Almería
Cartagena
Cabo de Palos
Cap de Creus
Cap de la Nau

BALEARIC ISLANDS
Palma
MALLORCA
MENORCA
EIVISSA

ITALY
Turin (Torino)
MILAN (MILANO)
Genoa (Genova)
Bologna
La Spezia
Livorno
Florence (Firenze)
Ancona
ROME (ROMA)
NAPLES (NAPOLI)
Bari
Taranto
Lecce
Cosenza
Catanzaro
Palermo
Messina
Catania
Cagliari
Sassari
Venice (Venezia)
SAN MARINO
MONACO
Nice
Ligurian Sea
Cap Corse
CORSICA (Fr.)
Ajaccio
SARDINIA (It.)
Capo Comino
Capo Carbonara
Capo Palinuro
SICILY (It.)
Mt. Etna
Capo Passero
Capo Colonna
Capo Spartivento

SLOVENIA
Ljubljana
CROATIA
Zagreb
BOSNIA AND HERZEGOVINA
Sarajevo
BELGRADE (BEOGRAD)
YUGOSLAVIA
ALBANIA
Tiranë

ADRIATIC SEA

TYRRHENIAN SEA
PANTELLERIA (It.)
Cap Bon
I. DI PANTELLERIA (It.)

IONIAN SEA

MEDITERRANEAN SEA

MALTA
Valletta

MOROCCO
Tanger
Tétouan
Ceuta (Sp.)
GIBRALTAR (U.K.)
Málaga
Melilla (Sp.)
Rabat
Meknès
Fès
CASABLANCA
Marrakech
Beni-Mellal
ATLAS MOUNTAINS

ALGERIA
ALGIERS (EL DJAZAÏR)
Wahran
Qacentina
Annaba
Batna
El Djelfa
Laghouat
Sousse

TUNISIA
Tunis
TUNIS

Strait of Gibraltar
Cádiz
Cabo de São Vicente

Scale 1:16,000,000; one inch to 252 miles
Lambert Conformal Conic Projection

ARCTIC OCEAN

ICELAND
Horn
Siglufjör-ur
GRIMSEY
Rifstangi
Fontur
Snæfellsnes
Brei-afjör-ur
Ísafjör-ur
Mýrasel
akflói
Mÿvatn
Reykjanes
Keflavik
Reykjavik
Selfoss
Thingvellir
Faxaflói
Hvannadalshnúkur
6.952 △
Prata
4.892 △
Vestmannaeyjar
Djúpivogur
Stokksnes

FAEROE
ISLANDS
(Den.)
Tórshavn

ATLANTIC
OCEAN

ROCKALL
(U.K.)

RONA

SHETLAND
ISLANDS
Lerwick
Sumburgh Head

SAINT
KILDA

ORKNEY
ISLANDS
Kirkwall
Duncansby Head
Wick

HEBRIDES
Stornoway
Cape Wrath
The Minch

BRITISH
ISLES

Bloody Foreland
Londonderry
Malin Head

NORTHERN
IRELAND
Ballymena
Belfast
Bangor

Donegal Bay
Erris Head
Achill Head

IRELAND
Clifden
Galway
Sligo
Dundalk

Loop Head
Kilkee
Tipperary
Dublin

Carrauntoohil
3.406 △
Tralee
Clonmel
Carlow
Waterford

Mizen
Head
Bantry
Kinsale
Cork
Dungarvan

CELTIC SEA

ISLES OF SCILLY

Inverness
Ben Nevis
4.406 △
GRAMPIAN MTS.
SCOTLAND
Aberdeen
Perth
Dundee

Tobermory
Moray Firth
Kinnaird Head

Kilmarnock
Glasgow
Stirling
CHEVIOT
HILLS
Edinburgh
Dumfries
Stranraer

ISLE OF MAN
(U.K.)
Douglas
Carlisle
Whitehaven

North Channel

Irish
Sea

St. George's Channel

Milford
Haven
Swansea
WALES
Cardiff
Newport

Hartland Point

Land's End
Penzance
Lizard Point

Saint Austell
Exeter
Start Point

Bloody Foreland

ENGLAND
Newcastle
upon Tyne
Sunderland
Middlesbrough
Scarborough

UNITED
GREAT
KINGDOM
BRITAIN
York
Kingston upon Hull
Grimsby

Liverpool
Chester
Manchester
Sheffield
Bradford
Stoke on Trent
Derby

Shrewsbury
Nottingham
Leicester
Norwich
BIRMINGHAM
Coventry
Northampton
Cambridge
Hereford
Great
Yarmouth

Oxford
Ipswich
Reading
LONDON

Southampton
Bournemouth
Portsmouth
Brighton

Strait of Dover

English Channel

Plymouth

Cap de la
Hague
Cherbourg
GUERNSEY
(U.K.)
CHANNEL IS.
JERSEY (U.K.)
Golfe de
Saint Malo

Pointe de Saint-Mathieu
Brest
Quimper
Pointe du Raz
Lorient

Dover

Le Havre
Dieppe
Abbeville

Calais
Lille
Lens

Brugge
Gent
BELGIUM
Brussels
(Bruxelles)
Antwerpen

NORTH
SEA

NETHERLANDS
Den Helder
Leeuwarden
Groningen

Haarlem
Amsterdam
Leiden
Utrecht
The Hague
('s-Gravenhage)
Rotterdam
Nijmegen
Tilburg

NORWEGIAN
SEA

Arctic Circle

Bodø

Mo

Mosjøen

Namsos
Steinkjer

Trondheim

Ålesund
Dombås
Galdhøpiggen
8.100 △

NORWAY
Lillehammer

Bergen
OSLO
Drammen
Lillestrøm
Skien
Sandefjord
Porsgrunn
Halden

Haugesund
Arendal

Stavanger
Lindesnes
Mandal
Kristiansand

Egersund

Skagerrak

Frederiks-
havn
Grenen

Göteborg
Borås

Varberg

SWEDEN
Sarna
Mora
Falun
Borlänge

Arvika
Karlstad

Säffle
Örebro

Trollhättan
Jönköping
Vetlanda

DENMARK
Hjørring
Ålborg
Viborg
Randers
Fornæs
Holstebro
Århus
Kolding
Esbjerg
Odense
SJÆLLAND
Copenhagen
(København)
Malmö
Trelleborg
Flensburg
Schleswig
LOLLAND
Nykøbing
Kiel

Cuxhaven
Wilhelmshaven
Bremerhaven
Oldenburg
Osnabrück
Münster
Dortmund
Essen
Wuppertal
Düsseldorf
Köln
Bonn
Siegen
Kassel
Koblenz
LUX.
Trier
Wiesbaden
Mainz
Frankfurt
Offenbach
Mannheim
Karlsruhe
Heidelberg
Würzburg
Saarbrücken
Heilbronn
Nürnberg

Namur
Liège
Maastricht
Mons
Charleroi
Luxembourg

Amiens
Saint
Quentin
Laon
Mézières
Reims

Rouen
Compiègne
Oise
Châlons-
sur-Marne
PARIS
Marne
Metz
Saint-Dizier

FRANCE
Caen
Évreux
Saint-Brieuc
Saint-Malo
Rennes
Laval
Le Mans
Chartres
Seine
Alençon
Vannes

Bailey lines / Sweden east side:
Na
LOFOTEN VESTERÅLEN

Sørs
Stormar
Vilhelmina
Åse
Östersund
Sollefte
Härnö
Strömsund
Bollnäs
Ljusdal
Leksand
Gävle
Uppsa
Västerås
Stock
Eskilstuna
Katrineholm
Norrk
Motala
Linköping
Västervik
Vetlanda
Ljungby
Kalmar
Värnamo
Oskarshamn
ÖLAN
Borg
Halmstad
Helsingborg
Karlshamn
Karlskrona
BORNHOLM
(Den.)
Rønne
Kap Arkona
BAL

GERMANY
HAMBURG
Bremen
Hannover
Bielefeld
Hildesheim
Braunschweig
Magdeburg
Göttingen
Dessau
Halle
Leipzig
Erfurt
Riesa
Dresden
Eisenach
Zwickau
Chemnitz
Coburg
Kladno
PRAGUE
(PRAHA)
CZECH REPUBLIC
Plzeň

Lübeck
Rostock
Schwerin
Neubrandenburg
Wittenberge
BERLIN
Potsdam
Fürstenwalde
Cottbus

Stralsund
Kołobrzeg
Świnoujście
Szczecin
Szczecinek
Stargard
Schwedt
Gorzów Wielkopol.
Poznań
Zielona Góra
Głogów
Legnica
Zary
Wałbrz
Liberec
Hradec
Králové
Olomouc

Kattegat

Copyright by Rand McNally & Co.
Made in U.S.A.
DM-559100-2A-QR1-·1·1·1

ATLANTIC OCEAN

CELTIC SEA

St. George's Channel

English Channel

NORTH SEA

Bay of Biscay

LIGURIAN SEA

TYRRHE SEA

MEDITE

IRELAND
NORTHERN IRELAND
UNITED KINGDOM
GREAT BRITAIN
ENGLAND
WALES
SCOTLAND
BRITISH ISLES

DENMARK
NETHERLANDS
BELGIUM
GERMANY
LUX.
FRANCE
SWITZERLAND
LIECHTENSTEIN

SPAIN
PORTUGAL
ANDORRA
PYRENEES
CORDILLERA CANTABRICA
SISTEMA IBERICO
SIERRA MORENA
SIERRA BÉTICA

CORSICA (Fr.)
SARDINIA (It.)
VATICAN CI
ROM
(ROM

MASSIF CENTRAL

MOROCCO
ALGERIA
TUNISIA
ATLAS MOUNTAINS
DAHRA

BALEARIC ISLANDS (Sp.)
MENORCA
MALLORCA
EIVISSA
FORMENTERA

ISOLA D'ELBA

Glasgow, Edinburgh, Belfast, Dublin, Liverpool, Manchester, Birmingham, London, Bristol, Cardiff, Nottingham, Sheffield, Leeds, Coventry, Leicester, Newcastle upon Tyne, Sunderland, Middlesbrough, York, Kingston upon Hull, Grimsby, Norwich, Cambridge, Oxford, Southampton, Portsmouth, Plymouth, Exeter, Bournemouth, Brighton, Dover, Reading

Copenhagen (København), Odense, Flensburg, Kiel, Lübeck, Hamburg, Bremen, Hannover, Amsterdam, The Hague ('s-Gravenhage), Rotterdam, Antwerpen, Brussel (Bruxelles), Köln, Bonn, Frankfurt, Wiesbaden, Mannheim, Stuttgart, München, Strasbourg, Karlsruhe, Nürnberg, Düsseldorf, Dortmund, Essen, Wuppertal, Münster

Paris, Le Havre, Cherbourg, Caen, Rennes, Nantes, Tours, Orléans, Bordeaux, Toulouse, Marseille, Lyon, Nice, Monaco, Grenoble, Dijon, Besançon, Limoges, Clermont-Ferrand, Saint-Étienne, Montpellier, Nîmes, Avignon, Toulon, Perpignan

Genève, Bern, Lausanne, Zürich, Luzern, Basel

Milan (MILANO), Turin (Torino), Genoa (Genova), Bologna, Verona, Parma, Modena, La Spezia, Livorno, Piacenza

La Coruña, Vigo, Porto, Lisbon (Lisboa), Madrid, Valladolid, Zaragoza, Barcelona, València, Sevilla, Córdoba, Granada, Málaga, Gibraltar (U.K.), Bilbao, Pamplona, Oviedo, Santander, Salamanca, Badajoz, Cádiz, Murcia, Alacant, Albacete, Palma

Tanger, Rabat, Casablanca, Meknes, Fès, Oujda, Algiers (EL DJAZAÏR), Wahran, Annaba, Tunis, Constantina, Batna

Scale 1:10,000,000; one inch to 158 miles
Lambert Conformal Conic Projection

12 125°
120°
10 115° 11 13 130° 14 135° 15 140° 16 145° 17 150° 18
B

Sosnovo-Ozerskoye
Chita
Shilka
Adinskoye
Borzya
Zabaykal'sk
Manzhouli
Sretensk
Shilka
Mohe
Gulian
Huma
Qiqian
WALL OF GENGHIS KHAN
Choybalsan
Baruun-Urt
Tamsagbulag
Hailar
Hulun Nur
GREATER KHINGAN RANGE
Butha Qi
Nunjiang
Bei'an
MANCHURIA
Komsomol'sk-na-Amure
Belogorsk
Blagoveshchensk
Svobodnyy
Raychikhinsk
Obluch'ye
Birobidzhan
Khabarovsk
SEA OF OKHOTSK
SAKHALIN
Pogranichnyy
Ussuriysk
Ol'ga
Svetlaya
Bikin
Dal'nerechensk
Lesozavodsk
Bel-negorsk
OSTROV SIMUSHIR
KURIL ISLANDS
45°
Krasnogorsk
Ugleporsk
Nevel'sk
Yuzhno-Sakhalinsk
Korsakov
OSTROV URUP
OSTROV ITURUP
The southern Kuril Islands are occupied by Russia pending a final peace treaty.
La Perouse Strait
Wakkanai
OSTROV KUNASHIR
C
150°

HEILONGJIANG
Yichun
Jiamusi
Hegang
Suihua
Jixi
Songhua
Anda
Hulan
HARBIN
Mudanjiang
QIQIHAR
Tongyu
Nunjiang
Baicheng
Nayoro
Mombetsu
Asahikawa
Rumoi
Kushiro
SAPPORO
Obihiro
HOKKAIDŌ
Otaru
Muroran
Hakodate
Erimo-misaki
40°

CHANGCHUN
JILIN
Huaide
Liaoyuan
JILIN
Shuanglao
Yanji
Najin
Ch'ŏngjin
Vladivostok
Nakhodka
Tsugaru Kaikyō
Aomori
Hachinohe
Hirosaki
Morioka
Kamaishi
35°

NEI MONGGOL
Abagner Qi
Abag Qi
Linxi
Duolun
Weichang
Chengde
Chaoyang
Tongliao
Kailu
Siping
Faku
Fuxin
SHENYANG
Benxi
LIAONING
Jinzhou
Liaoyang
ANSHAN
Yingkou
Tonghua
Kanggye
Hyesan
Kimch'aek
Tanch'ŏn
HONSHŪ
Akita
Sakata
Ishinomaki
Yamagata
Sendai
Niigata
Fukushima
Kōriyama
Iwaki
Hitachi
Nagaoka
Nagano
Utsunomiya
SEA OF JAPAN
D
17

Jining
Zhangjiakou
Xuanhua
GREAT WALL
Qinhuangdao
Dandong
Sinŭiju
Sunch'ŏn
Hamhŭng
Hŭngnam
Wŏnsan
NORTH KOREA
Kanggye
Toyama
Matsumoto
Kanazawa
Maebashi
TOKYO
Fukui
KAWASAKI
YOKOHAMA
NAGOYA
Mt. Fuji 12,388
JAPAN
145°

Datong
BEIJING
TANGSHAN
Hangu
TIANJIN
Lüshun
DALIAN
Korea Bay
Namp'o
P'YŎNGYANG
Kaesŏng
Haeju
SEOUL
(SŎUL)
INCH'ŎN
Suweon
Wŏnju
Kangnŭng
Sokch'o
Toyama
KYOTO
NARA
KOBE
OSAKA
Wakayama
Hamamatsu
E

Baoding
SHIJIAZHUANG
HEBEI
Yangquan
Yuci
Cangzhou
Huimin
Penglai
Weihai
Yantai
Shidao
Bo Hai
Chŏngju
TAEJON
TAEGU
P'ohang
Ulsan
OKI-SHOTŌ
Yonago
Tottori
HIROSHIMA
Kure
Takamatsu
Kōchi
SHIKOKU
30°

JINAN
SHANDONG
Dezhou
Zibo
Laiyang
Weifang
Boshan
QINGDAO
Tai'an
Xinwen
Yishui
Linyi
Yellow Sea
Kunsan
CHŎNJU
Masan
PUSAN
Chinju
Korea Strait
Shimonoseki
KITAKYŪSHŪ
Matsuyama
Ōita
FUKUOKA
Sasebo
Kumamoto
Miyazaki

Xinxiang
Kaifeng
ZHENGZHOU
Xuchang
Xuzhou
JIANGSU
Qingjiang
Yancheng
Binhai
KWANGJU
Mokp'o
Yŏsu
Cheju
CHEJU-DO (S. Korea)
KYŪSHŪ
Nagasaki
Kagoshima
Miyakonojō
Nishinoomote
TANEGA-SHIMA
16
F

HENAN
Bengbu
Huainan
Fuyang
Huangchuan
Yangzhou
Taizhou
Nantong
NANJING
Zhenjiang
Hefei
Changzhou
Wuxi
SHANGHAI
Wuhu
Suzhou
Jiaxing
YAKU-SHIMA
EAST CHINA SEA

WUHAN
Huangshi
HANGZHOU
Shaoxing
ZHEJIANG
Ningbo
Dinghai
RYUKYU ISLANDS (Japan)
Naze
AMAM-O-SHIMA
TOKUNO-SHIMA

CHANGSHA
Zhuzhou
Xiangtan
Pingxian
JIANGXI
Nanchang
Jingdezhen
Shangrao
Yingtan
Wenzhou
Pucheng
Rui'an
25°

Hengyang
Shaoyang
Ji'an
FUJIAN
Nanping
Luoyuan
Fuzhou
Nago
OKINAWA-JIMA
Naha
Tropic of Cancer
G

Chenxian
Suichuan
Ganzhou
Sanming
Mingqing
Putian
Chilung
T'AIPEI
Hsinchu
IRIOMOTE-JIMA
Hirara
MIYAKO-JIMA
ISHIGAKI-SHIMA
PACIFIC OCEAN
140°

Ruijin
Changting
Taichung
Hualien
Changhua
Chiai
20°

GUANGDONG
Meixian
Chao'an
Zhangzhou
Xiamen
Shantou
T'ainan
Shan 3,114
TAIWAN
KAOHSIUNG
Pingtung
T'AIWAN
Oluan Pi
OKINO-TORI-SHIMA (Japan)
H

GUANGZHOU
Foshan
Jiangmen
NEW KOWLOON
VICTORIA
MACAO (Port.)
HONG KONG (U.K.)
Luzon Strait
TUNGSHA TAO (Claimed by China, Taiwan)
SOUTH CHINA SEA
BABUYAN ISLANDS
Laoag
Aparri
PHILIPPINES
PHILIPPINE SEA
Copyright by Rand McNally & Co.
Made in U.S.A.
DM-569700-2A-QR1
15°

10 115° 11 120° 12 125° 13 130° 14 135° 15

Scale 1:16,000,000; one inch to 252 miles
Lambert Conformal Conic Projection

0 100 200 300 400 500 Miles
0 200 400 600 800 Kilometers

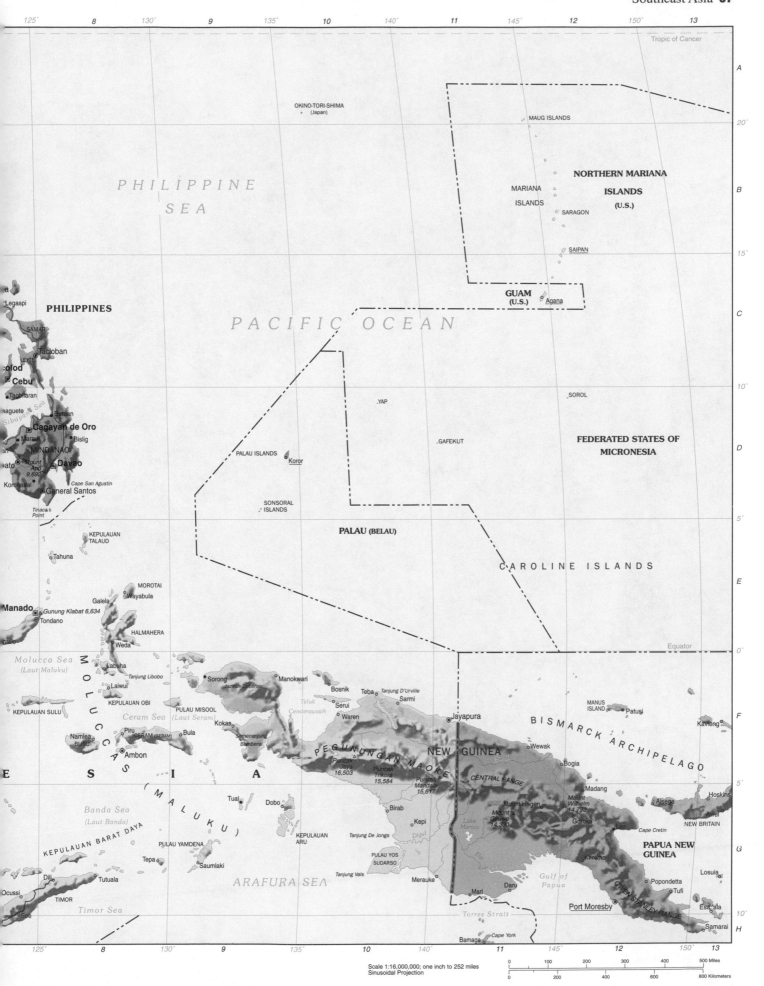

Tropic of Cancer

125°   8   130°   9   135°   10   140°   11   145°   12   150°   13

A

OKINO-TORI-SHIMA
(Japan)

MAUG ISLANDS

20°

NORTHERN MARIANA

B

P H I L I P P I N E

MARIANA
ISLANDS

ISLANDS
(U.S.)

S E A

SARAGON

15°

SAIPAN

GUAM
(U.S.) Agana

C

Legaspi

PHILIPPINES

P A C I F I C   O C E A N

SAMAR

LEYTE
Tacloban

.YAP

10°

olod **Cebu**

Tagbilaran

SOROL

aguete
Sibuyan Sea Butuan

.GAFEKUT

Cagayan de Oro

FEDERATED STATES OF
MICRONESIA

D

Maravii Bislig

PALAU ISLANDS Koror

MINDANAO

an
ato Mount
Apo **Davao**
9,692

Koronadai Cape San Agustin

General Santos

SONSORAL
ISLANDS

5°

Tinaca
Point

PALAU (BELAU)

KEPULAUAN
TALAUD

C A R O L I N E   I S L A N D S

E

Tahuna

MOROTAI
Wayabula

Manado Gunung Klabat 6,634
Tondano

Galela

HALMAHERA

Equator 0°

alo

Weda

Molucca Sea
(Laut Maluku)

Tanjung Libobo
Sorong

Manokwari

MANUS
ISLAND Patusi

Laiwui

Jazirah Doberai

Bosnik

Teba Tanjung D'Urville
Sarmi

B I S M A R C K   A R C H I P E L A G O

Kavieng

F

KEPULAUAN OBI

Serui

PULAU MISOOL
(Laut Seram)

Kokas

Waren

Ceram Sea

Teluk
Cenderawasih

Jayapura

KEPULAUAN SULU

Namlea
BURU Piru
CERAM (SERAM) Bula

NEW GUINEA

Wewak

Bogia

Madang Aisega

Hoskins

Ambon

E **S** **I**

Somenanjung
Bemberai Puncak
Jaya
16,503 Puncak
Trikora
15,584 Puncak
Mandala
15,617 **CENTRAL RANGE**

Mount Hagen
Goroka

Mount Wilhelm
14,793

NEW BRITAIN

A

Tual

Dobo

Birab

Mount a
Giluwe
14,330

Cape Cretin

Awul

5°

Banda Sea
(Laut Banda)

Kepi

Lake
Murray

Kerema

Losuia

Tepa

KEPULAUAN
ARU

Tanjung De Jongs

Digul

Fly

Popondetta

Tufi

G

KEPULAUAN BARAT DAYA

PULAU YAMDENA

Saumlaki

PULAU YOS
SUDARSO

PAPUA NEW
GUINEA

Dili Tutuala

Saumlaki

Tanjung Vals

A R A F U R A   S E A

Merauke

Mari

Daru

Gulf of
Papua

Esa ala

Samarai

Ocussi
Soe TIMOR

Timor Sea

Port Moresby

10°

Torres Strait

Bamaga Cape York

H

125°   8   130°   9   135°   10   140°   11   145°   12   150°   13

Scale 1:16,000,000; one inch to 252 miles
Sinusoidal Projection

0 100 200 300 400 500 Miles

0 200 400 600 800 Kilometers

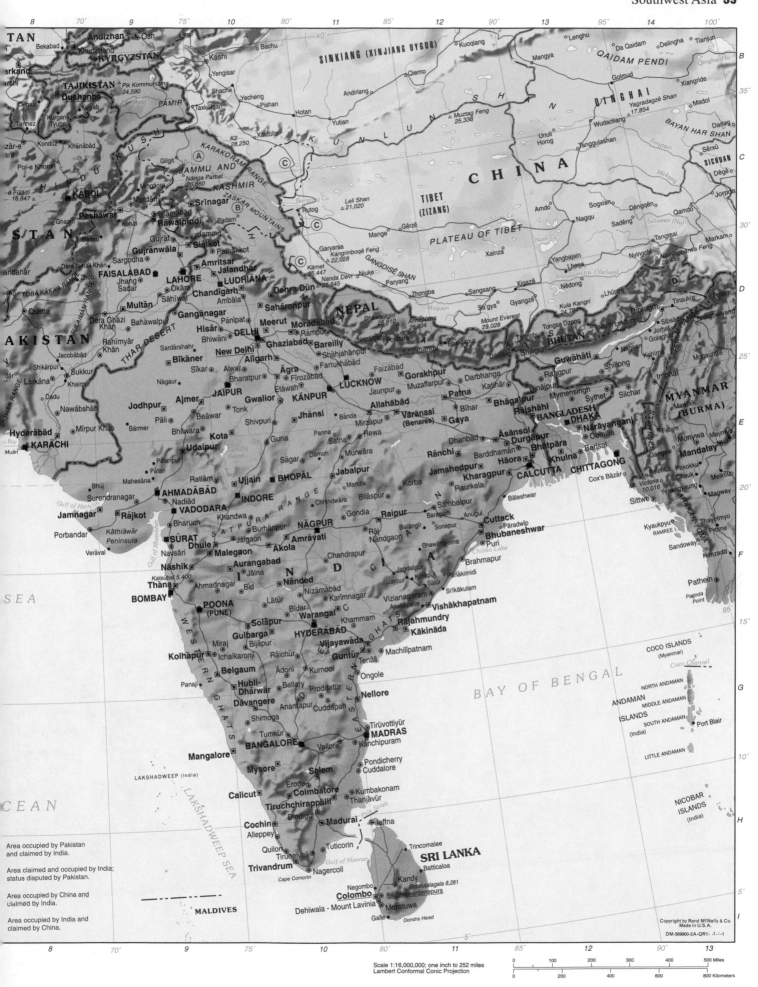

Scale 1:16,000,000; one inch to 252 miles
Lambert Conformal Conic Projection

0   100   200   300   400   500 Miles

0   200   400   600   800 Kilometers

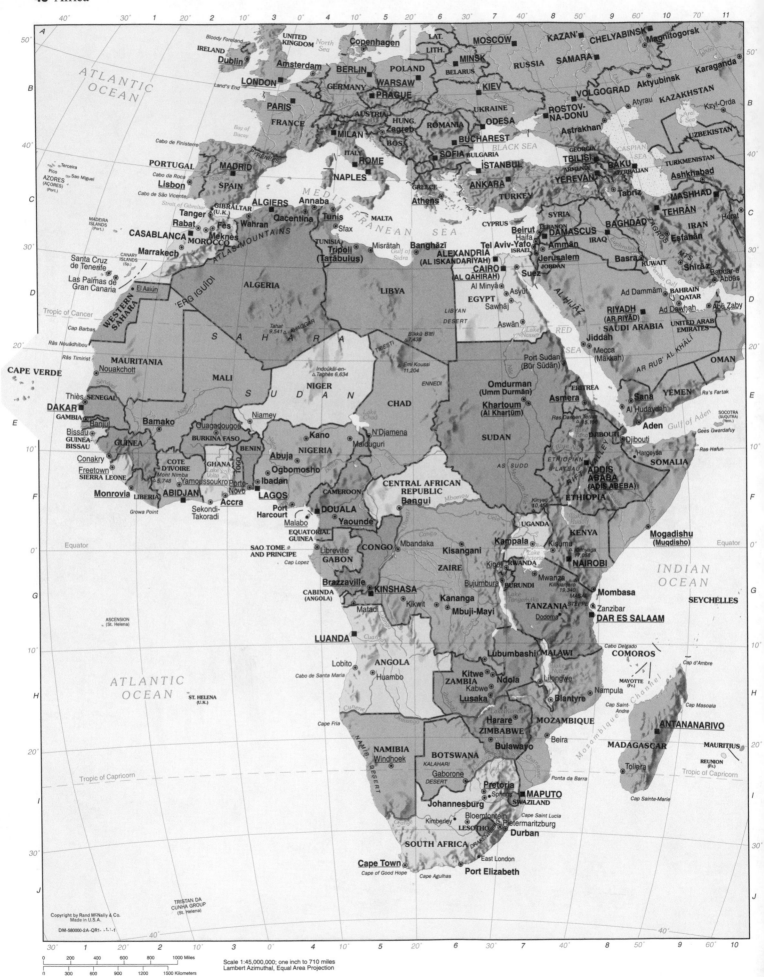

Scale 1:45,000,000; one inch to 710 miles
Lambert Azimuthal, Equal Area Projection

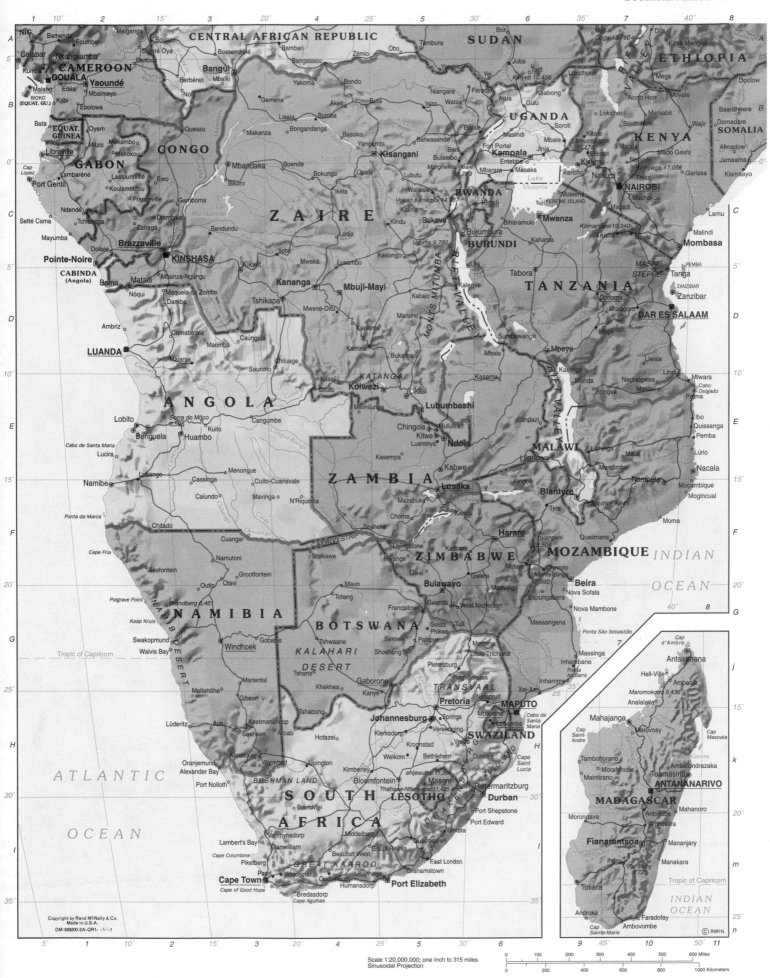

Scale 1:20,000,000; one inch to 315 miles
Sinusoidal Projection

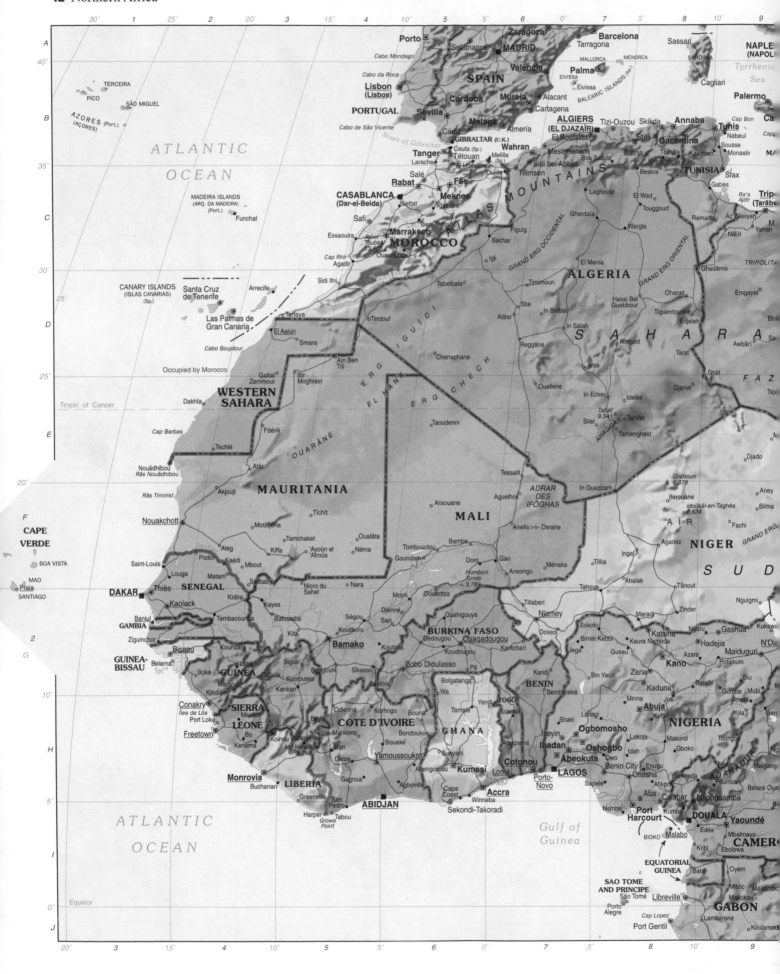

ATLANTIC OCEAN

AZORES (Port.)
(AÇORES)

TERCEIRA

PICO

SÃO MIGUEL

MADEIRA ISLANDS
(ARQ. DA MADEIRA)
(Port.)

Funchal

CANARY ISLANDS
(ISLAS CANARIAS)
(Sp.)

Santa Cruz
de Tenerife

Las Palmas de
Gran Canaria

Arrecife

Tropic of Cancer

Cap Barbas

CAPE VERDE

BOA VISTA

MAO

Praia
SANTIAGO

ATLANTIC OCEAN

Porto

Cabo Mondego

Cabo da Roca

Lisbon
(Lisboa)

PORTUGAL

Sevilla

Cabo de São Vicente

Strait of Gibraltar

GIBRALTAR (U.K.)

Tanger

Larache

Salé

Rabat

CASABLANCA
(Dar-el-Beida)

Settat

Safi

Essaouira

Marrakech

Jebel
Toubkal
13,665

Cap Rhir

Agadir

Sidi Ifni

Ben-Mellal

Tarfaya

El Aaiún

Smara

Cabo Bojdour

WESTERN SAHARA

Dakhla

Occupied by Morocco

Galtat
Zemmour

Fdérik

Techlé

Nouâdhibou
Râs Nouâdhibou

Atâr

Râs Timiris

Akjoujt

MAURITANIA

Nouakchott

Moudjeria

Tîchît

Saint-Louis

Aleg

Kiffa

Tamchaket

'Ayoûn el
'Atroûs

Néma

Oualâta

Louga

Podor

Kaédi

Mbout

DAKAR

Thiès

SENEGAL

Kaolack

Matam

Sélibaby

Nioro du
Sahel

Nara

Kidira

Banjul

GAMBIA

Kayes

Bafoulabé

Kita

Tambacounda

Ziguinchor

Bissau

GUINEA-BISSAU

Bolama

Bamako

Koulikoro

Koutiala

Bolama

Boké

Koundara

Labé

GUINEA

Siguiri

Bougouni

Sikasso

Conakry

Îles de Lós
Port Loko

Mamou

Dabola

Kouroussa

Kankan

Beyla

BURKINA FASO

Bobo Dioulasso

Banfora

SIERRA LEONE

Makeni

Bo

Kenema

Koindu
Nzérékoré

Mt. Nimba
5,748

Man

Odienné

Korhogo

Bouna

Mankono

CÔTE D'IVOIRE

Bouaké

Yamoussoukro

Freetown

Monrovia

Buchanan

LIBERIA

Daloa

Gagnoa

Greenville

San Pédro

Harper

Growa
Point

Tabou

Sunyani

GHANA

Kumasi

Abengourou

Agboville

ABIDJAN

Sekondi-Takoradi

Cape Coast

Winneba

Accra

SPAIN

MADRID

Salamanca

Córdoba

Málaga

Cádiz

Almería

Ceuta (Sp.)

Tétouan

Melilla
(Sp.)

Al Hoceima

Oujda

Fès

Meknès

Khenifra

Khouribga

Figuig

Béchar

Igli

Oued Draa

Tindouf

Ain Ben
Tili

Bir
Moghrein

EL HANK

ERG IGUIDI

ERG CHECH

OUARÂNE

Tessalit

Araouane

Tombouctou

Goundam

Bamba

Gao

Doro

Ansongo

Hombori
Tondo
3,789

Ménaka

Mopti

Douentza

Djenné

San

Ségou

Ouahigouya

Bédougou

Ouagadougou

Koudougou

Pô

Kantchari

Koutiala

MALI

Aguelhok

ADRAR DES IFÔGHAS

Anefis i-n- Darane

Zaragoza

Tarragona

Barcelona

MALLORCA

MENORCA

BALEARIC ISLANDS (Sp.)

EIVISSA

Palma

Eivissa

Cagliari

Valencia

Murcia

Alacant

Cartagena

ALGIERS
(EL DJAZAÏR)

Tizi-Ouzou

Skikda

Annaba

Tunis

El Boulaida

Mostaganem

Bou Saâda

Batna

Tbessa

Stif

Qacentina

Beskra

Khenchla

TUNISIA

Sfax

Gabès

Sousse

Monastir

Kairouan

Wahran

Sidi bel Abbès

Tillimsen

Saïda

Laghouat

El Wad

Touggourt

GRAND ERG OCCIDENTAL

Ghardaïa

Wargla

GRAND ERG ORIENTAL

Ghadâmis

El Menia

Timimoun

Tabelbala

Sba

In Belbel

Adrar

Hassi Bel
Guebbour

Ohanet

Emgayet

Reggâne

In Salah

Amguid

Tiguentourine

Edjeleh

Chenachane

Ouallene

In Ecker

Idelès

Tarat

Djanet

Taoudenni

Silet

Tahat
9,541

Ahaggar

Tahifet

Tamenghest

ALGERIA

SAHARA

In Guezzam

Gréboun
6,378

Iferouane

Djado

Idoukâl-en-Taghès
6,634

Aney

Bilma

AÏR

Agadez

Fachi

NIGER

Tillia

Ingal

Abalak

Tahoua

Tânout

Tillabéri

Niamey

Dosso

Sokoto

Birnin Kebbi

Gusau

Katsina

Maradi

Zinder

Ngouru

Gashua

Maïduguri

Potiskum

Kano

Zaria

Kaduna

Hadejia

Katsina

Kaura Namoda

Bin Yauri

Kandi

BENIN

Bembèrèké

Kontcha

Abuja

Wa

Bolgatanga

Yendi

TOGO

Sokodé

Lafiagi

Shaki

Iseyin

Minna

Jos

NIGERIA

Tamale

Atakpamé

Lokoja

Makurdi

Ogbomosho

Oshogbo

Ibadan

Abeokuta

Owo

Benin City

Onitsha

Cotonou

Porto-Novo

LAGOS

Sapele

Enugu

Abakaliki

Calabar

Lomé

Aba

DOUALA

Yaoundé

Port Harcourt

Kumba

BIOKO

Malabo

EQUATORIAL GUINEA

Bata

Oyem

SAO TOME AND PRINCIPE

São Tomé

Libreville

GABON

Porto Alegre

Cap Lopez

Port Gentil

Lambaréné

Koulamoutou

Gulf of Guinea

Equator

Scale 1:20,000,000; one inch to 315 miles
Sinusoidal Projection

0 100 200 300 400 500 600 Miles

0 200 400 600 800 1000 Kilometers

PACIFIC

RUSSIA
SEA OF OKHOTSK
BERING SEA
SAKHALIN
Poluostrov Kamchatka
KURIL ISLANDS
International Date Line
ALEUTIAN IS.

HOKKAIDO
Vladivostok
SAPPORO
SEA OF JAPAN
JAPAN
HONSHŪ
Fuji-san 12,388
TŌKYŌ
YOKOHAMA
KYŪSHŪ
KITAKYŪSHŪ
KŌBE
PUSAN

BEIJING
SHENYANG
NORTH KOREA
PYŎNGYANG
SEOUL
SOUTH KOREA
QINGDAO
TIANJIN
XI'AN
WUHAN
NANJING
SHANGHAI
Chongqing
CHINA
Yangtze
HIMALAYAS
Kathmandu
NEPAL
BHU.
INDIA
BNGL.
CHITTAGONG
MYANMAR (BURMA)
LAOS
Ha Noi
MACAO (Port.)
Hai Phong
GUANGZHOU
HONG KONG (U.K.)
T'AIPEI
TAIWAN
KAOHSIUNG
HAINAN DAO
Viangchan
YANGON
THAILAND
BANGKOK
CAMBODIA
VIETNAM
Da Nang
SOUTH CHINA SEA
Mekong

Tropic of Cancer

PHILIPPINE SEA
Escarpada Point
LUZON
MANILA
QUEZON CITY
PHILIPPINES
Cebu
Zamboanga
MINDANAO
Davao
Gunong Kinabalu 13,455

MICRONESIA

NORTHERN MARIANA ISLANDS (U.S.)
MARIANA ISLANDS
GUAM (U.S.)

MARSHALL ISLANDS

Phnum Pénh
THANH PHO HO CHI MINH (SAIGON)
Mui Ca Mau
MALAYSIA
Bandar Seri Begawan
BRUNEI
KUALA LUMPUR
SINGAPORE
Koror
PALAU ISLANDS
FEDERATED STATES OF MICRONESIA

PALAU (BELAU)
CAROLINE ISLANDS
KIRIBATI

Equator
BORNEO (KALIMANTAN)
Gunung Kerinci 12,467
SUMATRA
PALEMBANG
Banjarmasin
CELEBES
CERAM
JAKARTA
SURABAYA
JAVA
INDONESIA
Puncak Jaya 16,503
Mt. Giluwe 14,330
NEW GUINEA
NEW BRITAIN
PAPUA NEW GUINEA
Port Moresby
BOUGAINVILLE
Honiara
SOLOMON ISLANDS
MELANESIA
TUVALU

NAURU
PHOENIX
KIR
KIR
TOK
TOK

Tanjung Vals
TIMOR
ARAFURA SEA
Cape York
SANTA CRUZ ISLANDS
WALLIS AND FUTUNA (Fr.)
WEST
SAM

CHRISTMAS ISLAND (Austl.)
TIMOR SEA
Cape Londonderry
Darwin
Gulf of Carpentaria
Cape York Peninsula
CORAL SEA
VANUATU
NEW CALEDONIA (Fr.)
Port Vila
FIJI
VANUA LEVU
VITI LEVU
Suva
TON

Cape Leveque
Normanton
Cooktown
Cairns
Townsville
GREAT DIVIDING RANGE
NOUVELLE CALÉDONIE
Nouméa

INDIAN OCEAN
Cape Capricorn
NORFOLK ISLAND (Austl.)
GREAT SANDY DESERT
North West Cape
Alice Springs
Sandy Cape
Carnarvon
Carnegie
△ Ayers Rock 2,844
AUSTRALIA
Brisbane

Tropic of Capricorn
GREAT VICTORIA DESERT
Darling
Newcastle
GREAT DIVIDING RANGE
Sydney
North Cape
Auckland
NORTH ISLAND
East Cape
Mt. Ruapehu 9,177
Kalgoorlie-Boulder
Port Augusta
Canberra
TASMAN SEA
Wanneroo
Perth
Great Australian Bight
Cape Arid
Cape Carnot
Adelaide
Mt. Kosciusko 7,310
Cape Howe
Cape Farewell
Wellington
NEW ZEALAND
Christchurch
SOUTH ISLAND
Cape Naturaliste
Hood Point
Cape Jaffa
Melbourne
Cape Otway
Cape Grim
Cape Portland
Point D'Entrecasteaux
TASMANIA
Mt. Ossa 5,305
Hobart
South East Cape
Mt. Cook 12,316
Cape Providence
STEWART ISLAND
CHATHAM ISLA

12 160° 13 150° 14 140° 15 16 130° 17 110° 18 100° 19 90° 20 80° 21 70° 22

UNITED STATES
VANCOUVER ISLAND
Seattle
Portland
ROCKY MOUNTAINS
Denver
St. Louis
Cape Fear
ATLANTIC OCEAN
30°

SIERRA NEVADA
San Francisco
UNITED STATES
Memphis
Atlanta
APPALACHIAN MOUNTAINS
Jacksonville

Albuquerque
DALLAS
Mississippi
Cape Canaveral
D
70°

Los Angeles
San Diego
Tucson
El Paso
San Antonio
HOUSTON
Tampa
Miami
BAHAMAS

OCEAN

Punta Eugenia
Baja California
MONTERREY
HAVANA
CUBA
20°

MEXICO
Tampico
Mérida
Yucatán Peninsula
CARIBBEAN SEA
JAMAICA
Kingston

San Luis Potosí
Gulf of Mexico
Cape Sable

Tropic of Cancer
Cabo San Lucas
GUADALAJARA
MEXICO CITY
PUEBLA
BELIZE

HAWAIIAN ISLANDS (U.S.)
OAHU
MAUI
Honolulu
HAWAII
Hilo
Acapulco
GUATEMALA
GUATEMALA
HONDURAS
Tegucigalpa

EL SALVADOR
San Salvador
NICARAGUA

Managua
COSTA RICA
San José
80°
10°

F

LINE ISLANDS
POLYNESIA
Equator
GALAPAGOS ISLANDS (ARCHIPIÉLAGO DE COLÓN) (Ecuador)
Punta Galera
0°
80°
QUITO
ECUADOR
GUAYAQUIL

I
NORTHERN COOK ISLANDS
MARQUESAS ISLANDS (ÎLES MARQUISES)
Punta Pariñas
Chiclayo
PERU
ANDES

AMERICAN SAMOA
COOK ISLANDS (N.Z.)
TUAMOTU ARCHIPELAGO
FRENCH POLYNESIA
Nev. Huascarán 22,133

Papeete
TAHITI
Punta Lachay
Callao
Lima

SOUTHERN COOK ISLANDS
Punta Carreta

Punta Parada
PITCAIRN (U.K.)
Tropic of Capricorn
20°
Arequipa

EASTER ISLAND (ISLA DE PASCUA) (Chile)

PACIFIC OCEAN
CHILE
ARGENTINA

Valparaíso
CÓRDOBA
Santiago
40°
30°

12 160° 13 150° 14 140° 15 130° 16 120° 17 110° 18 100° 19 90° 20 80° 21 70° 22 60°

Scale 1:45,000,000; one inch to 710 miles
Lambert Azimuthal, Equal Area Projection

0 200 400 600 800 1000 Miles

0 300 600 900 1200 1500 Kilometers

SOLOMON SEA

NEW BRITAIN

Lae

Cape Cretin

BOUGAINVILLE

Popondetta

Kulumadau

CHOISEUL

SANTA ISABEL

SOLOMON
ISLANDS

Samarai

Honiara

MALAITA

GUADALCANAL

SAN CRISTOBAL

TUVALU

CORAL SEA

SANTA CRUZ
ISLANDS

ÎLES BANKS

VANUATU

WALLIS
AND
FUTUNA
(Fr.)

ESPIRITU SANTO

PENTECATE

MALAKULA

EPI

Port Vila

ÉFATÉ

NEW

FIJI

VANUA
LEVU

Lautoka

VITI
LEVU

Suva

ERROMANGO

NEW
CALEDONIA
(Fr.)

NOUVELLE
CALÉDONIE

HEBRIDES

KANDUVU
ISLAND

LOYALTY
ISLANDS

Nouméa

PACIFIC

OCEAN

Tropic of Capricorn

Townsville

Halifax Bay

Mackay

Mt. Dalrymple
4,131

Blair Athol

Rockhampton

Cape Capricorn

Emerald

Gladstone

Springsure

Theodore

Bundaberg

Maryborough

Sandy Cape

FRASER ISLAND

Mitchell

Gympie

Mt. Kiangarow
3,760

Chinchilla

Redcliffe

Teowoomba

Brisbane

Ipswich

DARLING
DOWNS

Southport

Warwick

Cape Byron

Armidale

Grafton

Nyngan

Tamworth

Coffs
Harbour

Dubbo

Taree

WALES

Cessnock

Newcastle

Penrith

Parramatta

Goulburn

Sydney

Campbelltown

Wollongong

A.C.T.

Canberra

Jervis Bay

Cooma

Mt. Kosciusko
7,310

Cape Howe

NORFOLK ISLAND
(Austl.)

Sale

TASMAN

Wilsons Promontory

SEA

FLINDERS ISLAND

Cape Portland

Devonport

Launceston

Freycinet Peninsula

TASMANIA

South East Cape

Cape Maria
van Diemen

North
Cape

Cape Brett

Whangarei

Needles Point

Mount Roskill

East Coast Bays

Auckland

Manukau

Hamilton

Bay of Plenty

Tauranga

Albatross Point

NORTH ISLAND

East Cape

New Plymouth

Taupo

Rotorua

Cape
Egmont

Mt. Ruapehu
9,175

Wanganui

Gisborne

Cape Farewell

Palmerston North

Napier

The Twins
5,980

Hastings

Nelson

Greymouth

Porirua

SOUTH ISLAND

Wellington

Haast

NEW
ZEALAND

Jackson Head

SOUTHERN ALPS

Wanaka

Christchurch

Ashburton

West Cape

Timaru

CHATHAM
ISLANDS
(N.Z.)

Oamaru

Invercargill

Foveaux Strait

Dunedin

STEWART
ISLAND

Scale 1:20,000,000; one inch to 315 miles
Lambert's Azimuthal; Equal Area Projection

0   100   200   300   400   500   600 Miles

0   200   400   600   800   1000 Kilometers

PACIFIC OCEAN

ARGENTINA

CHILE

Rosario

BUENOS AIRES

URUGUAY
MONTEVIDEO

BRAZIL

Rio de la Plata

ARCHIPIÉLAGO
DE LOS
CHONOS

Strait of
Magellan

TIERRA
DEL
FUEGO

FALKLAND ISLANDS
(U.K.)

Cape Horn

DRAKE PASSAGE

Scotia Sea

ATLANTIC OCEAN

SOUTH GEORGIA
(U.K.)

SOUTH SHETLAND
ISLANDS (U.K.)

Palmer
Station
(U.S.)

ADELAIDE I.

Bellingshausen
Sea

Antarctic Circle

ALEXANDER I.

LARSEN
ICE SHELF

SOUTH ORKNEY
ISLANDS (U.K.)

SOUTH SANDWICH
ISLANDS (U.K.)

THURSTON I.

Amundsen
Sea

Mt. Rexi
3,625

RONNE
ICE SHELF

Weddell Sea

Mt. Siple
10,203

Mt. Sidley
13,717

Mt. Ulmer
8,996

Vinson Massif
16,066

ELLSWORTH
MTS.

BERKNER I.

MARIE
BYRD
LAND

WHITMORE
MTS.

FILCHNER
ICE SHELF

COATS
LAND

ROCKEFELLER
PLATEAU

PENSACOLA
MTS.

Cape
Norvegia

THIEL
MTS.

QUEEN
MAUD
MTS.

QUEEN MAUD LAND

MÜHLIG
HOFMANN
MTS.

ROOSEVELT I.

Ross
Sea

ROSS ICE
SHELF

Amundsen - Scott
South Pole Station
(U.S.)

South Pole

Mt. Markham
14,049

Mt. Albert Markham
10,522

SØR RONDANE
MTS.

McMurdo Station (U.S.)

Cape
Adare

Mt. Erebus
12,451

Mt. Minto 13,658

Mt. McClintock
11,457

ANTARCTICA

TRANSANTARCTIC MOUNTAINS

QUEEN FABIOLA
MTS.

CAMPBELL I. (N.Z.)

VICTORIA LAND

AUCKLAND IS.
(N.Z.)

ENDERBY
LAND

GEORGE V COAST

MACQUARIE ISLAND
(Austl.)

AMERICAN
HIGHLAND

NAPIER MTS.

Cape
Ann

South Magnetic Pole

WILKES LAND

AMERY
ICE SHELF

Cape
Darnley

Antarctic Circle

PRINCE
EDWARD IS.
(S. Afr.)

Cape
Poinsett

ARCHIPEL
CROZET
(Fr.)

HEARD ISLAND
(Austl.)

ÎLES KERGUÉLEN
(Fr.)

INDIAN OCEAN

Great Australian Bight

AUSTRALIA

0   200   400   600   800   1000 Miles

0   300   600   900   1200   1500 Kilometers

Scale 1:45,000,000; one inch to 710 miles
Polar Sterographic Projection

Index

Abbreviations of Geographical Names and Terms

Ab., Can. .... Alberta
Ak., U.S. .... Alaska
Al., U.S. .... Alabama
Ant. .... Antarctica
Ar., U.S. .... Arkansas
Arg. .... Argentina
Asia .... Asia
Austl............. Australia
Az., U.S. .... Arizona

b............. bay, gulf
Bah. .... Bahrain
B.C., Can. ...... British Columbia
Bol.............Bolivia
Braz. ....Brazil

c.........cape, point
Ca., U.S. .... California
Can. .... Canada
Cay.Is.....Cayman Islands
C.Iv. .... Cote d'Ivoire
Co., U.S. .... Colorado
Col. .... Colombia
cont...... continent

C.R. ....Costa Rica
Ct., U.S. .....Connecticut
ctry. .... country

D.C., U.S. ...... District of Columbia
De., U.S. .... Delaware
dep. .... dependency
Dom. Rep. ...... Dominican Republic

El Sal. .... El Salvador
Eng., U.K. .... England
Eur. ....Europe

Falk. Is. ....Falkland Islands
Fl., U.S. ....Florida

Ga., U.S. .... Georgia
Guad. ....Guadeloupe

hist. reg.....historic region
H.K.......... Hong Kong
Hond. .... Honduras

i. ....island
Ia., U.S. .... Iowa
Id., U.S. .... Idaho
Il., U.S. .... Illinois
In., U.S. .... Indiana
Indon........... Indonesia
I. of Man .... Isle of Man
Ire. ....Ireland
is. .... islands

Jam.............Jamaica

Ks., U.S. ....Kansas
Ky., U.S. .... Kentucky

l. ....lake
La., U.S. .... Louisiana
Leb. .... Lebanon

Ma., U.S. ... Massachusetts
Malay...........Malaysia
Md., U.S. ...... Maryland
Me., U.S. .... Maine
Mex.............. Mexico
Mi., U.S. .... Michigan

Mn., U.S. .... Minnesota
Mo., U.S. .... Missouri
Mong. .... Mongolia
Monts........Montserrat
Mor...........Morocco
Moz..........Mozambique
Ms., U.S. .... Mississippi
Mt., U.S. .... Montana
mth. ....river mouth
mtn. .... mountain
mts. .... mountains

N.A. ......North America
Nb., U.S. .... Nebraska
N.B., Can. ...... New Brunswick
N.C., U.S. ...... North Carolina
N.D., U.S. ...North Dakota
Newf., Can. ...... Newfoundland
N.H., U.S. ...... New Hampshire
Nic. ....Nicaragua

N. Ire., U.K. ...... Northern Ireland
N.J., U.S. .... New Jersey
N.M., U.S. ... New Mexico
N.S., Can. ... Nova Scotia
Nv., U.S. .... Nevada
N.W.T., Can. ...... Northwest Territories
N.Y., U.S. .... New York
N.Z. .... New Zealand

Oh., U.S. ....Ohio
Ok., U.S. .... Oklahoma
Ont., Can. .... Ontario
Or., U.S. .... Oregon

Pa., U.S. .... Pennsylvania
Pak. .... Pakistan
Pan. .... Panama
Para. .... Paraguay
pen. .... peninsula
Phil. .... Philippines
plat. ....plateau
pol. div... political division
Port............ Portugal

P.R. ....Puerto Rico
prov............. province

Que., Can........ Quebec

res. .... reservoir

S. Africa .... South Africa
Sask., Can. ...... Saskatchewan

S.C., U.S. ...... South Carolina
Scot., U.K. ...... Scotland
S.D., U.S. ... South Dakota
Sen. .... Senegal
Sri L. .... Sri Lanka
St. K./N. ...... St. Kitts and Nevis
stm. .... river, stream
strt..............strait

terr............territory
Tn., U.S. .... Tennessee
Trin. ...... Trinidad and Tobago

Tx., U.S. .... Texas

U.K......United Kingdom
Urug............ Uruguay
U.S. .... United States
Ut., U.S. ....Utah

Va., U.S. ....Virginia
Ven. .... Venezuela
vol. .... volcano
Vt., U.S. ....Vermont

Wa., U.S. ..... Washington
W. Bank ...... West Bank
Wi., U.S. .... Wisconsin
W.V., U.S... West Virginia
Wy., U.S. .... Wyoming

T